HOW TO PARTNER WITH GIRL SCOUT SENIORS ON

MISSION: SISTERHOOD!

IT'S YOUR STORY—TELL IT! A LEADERSHIP JOURNEY

Girl Scouts of the USA

CHAIR,
NATIONAL BOARD
OF DIRECTORS
Connie L. Lindsey

CHIEF
EXECUTIVE
OFFICER
Kathy Cloninger

CHIEF OPERATING
OFFICER
Jan Verhage

VICE PRESIDENT,
PROGRAM
Eileen Doyle

WRITTEN BY Andrea Bastiani Archibald,
Laura J. Tuchman, and Valerie Takahama

CONTRIBUTOR: Tommi Lewis Tilden

ILLUSTRATED BY Susy Pilgrim Waters

DESIGNED BY Emily Peterson and Sheryl O'Connell

EXECUTIVE EDITOR: Laura J. Tuchman

PROGRAM TEAM: Douglas Bantz, Ellen Kelliher,
Sarah Micklem, Sheryl O'Connell, Lesley Williams

DIRECTOR, PROGRAM RESOURCES: Suzanne Harper

© 2010 by Girl Scouts of the USA

First published in 2010 by Girl Scouts of the USA
420 Fifth Avenue, New York, NY 10018-2798
www.girlscouts.org

ISBN: 978-0-88441-759-0

All rights reserved. Except for pages intended for reuse by Girl Scout volunteers, this book may not be reproduced in whole or in part in any form or by any means, electronic or mechanical, including photocopying, recording, or by any information storage or retrieval system now known or hereafter invented, without the prior written permission of Girl Scouts of the United States of America.

Printed in Italy

1 2 3 4 5 6 7 8 9/17 16 15 14 13 12 11 10

CREDIT: Pages 72 and 73, Buddy Button Bracelets by Kimberley Stoney

This publication was made possible by a generous grant from the Dove Self-Esteem Fund.

Text printed on Fedrigoni Cento 40 percent de-inked, post-consumer fibers and 60 percent secondary recycled fibers. Covers printed on Prisma artboard FSC Certified mixed sources.

CONTENTS

BUILDING GIRLS' CONFIDENCE 4

What to Pack for the Journey 6

Stories + Creativity = 2 Fun Ways to Build Girls' Leadership 8

Why Self-Esteem Matters! 10

Session Plans Make the Most of Seniors' Skills 11

The Sisterhood Award 12

Ladder of Leadership 13

What You'll Find in Each Sample Session Plan 14

Creating a Network of Journey Resources 16

Girl Scout Traditions and Ceremonies 18

Keys to Girl Leadership 20

How Girls Have Fun in Girl Scouts 21

What It All Means for Girls 22

Your Perspective on Leadership 25

THE SAMPLE SESSION PLANS 26

Journey Snapshot 27

Session 1: Starting Our Sisterhood 28

Session 2: Know Thyself 36

Session 3: With Friends Like These 44

Session 4: Your Mission Starts Now! 54

Session 5: Fit for the Mission 60

Sessions 6 & 7: Sisterhood Knows No Boundaries 66

Session 8: Making Sisterhood Your Story! 76

Sessions 9 & 10: Celebrating the Circle of Sisterhood 80

Building girls' confidence is the goal of this *It's Your Story—Tell It* journey.

Building **confidence** every day.

Girl Scouting builds girls of **courage**, **confidence**, and character, who make the world a better place.

That's our **mission**. And we do it through 3 keys to leadership: **Discover + Connect + Take Action**

On this journey…

Girl Scout Seniors realize the benefits of sisterhood—for themselves and the world.

They also learn ways to broaden their friendship borders—and be their own best friend.

Sisterhood—it strengthens girls and it strengthens the world!

Imagine how far a Senior can go and how much she can do—for herself and the world—when she has confidence *and* sisterhood.

There are more than 3 million teen girls in 9th and 10th grade across the country. Imagine all of them as Girl Scout Seniors on this leadership journey, Discovering, Connecting, and Taking Action. Now, that's a powerful sisterhood!

What to pack for the journey!

Girl Scout leadership journeys invite girls to explore a theme through many experiences and from many perspectives—through the 3 keys to leadership: **Discover + Connect + Take Action**

All the joys of travel are built right in! So fill your suitcase with everything you need for an amazing trip that will change girls' lives!

The Girls' Book

Exciting challenges, real-life stories, and creative projects, let girls . . . meet new people, explore new things, make memories, earn a leadership award, and have fun—all while exploring a theme through the 3 keys to leadership!

The Adult Guide

Fun and easy activities to get girls thinking and doing while team-building and getting creative—as they explore the 3 keys to leadership! Plus: healthful snacks and loads of tips for engaging girls in leadership.

Your Wider Community

Women in all career fields, and experts in storytelling and the arts. Local partners: museums, arts groups, professional associations, colleges, and libraries.

Your Enthusiasm

And your interests and talents, your partnership with girls and families, and, most important, your willingness to learn by doing, right alongside the girls!

Stories + Creativity = 2 Fun Ways to Build Girls' Leadership

This Girl Scout leadership journey is part of a series that invites girls into the fun and friendly world of storytelling.

Stories are fundamental to how girls learn about themselves and the world.

Stories allow girls to absorb the ideas and richness of many cultures, and that develops their empathy, tolerance, and acceptance of others.

Stories sharpen girls' minds and spark their imaginations.

Stories inspire and motivate.

Stories teach girls how to lead and keep them growing as leaders.

Stories of Sisterhood! From real sisters working out together to a sisterhood of women working for change, this journey is sprinkled with stories of sisterhood and the benefits they bring to women and the world. The Seniors gain personal inspiration from these stories and also an understanding that with sisterhood behind them they can change the world.

A book for every girl! So that girls can enjoy the journey whenever they like, it's important that all girls have their own journey book. They can draw inspiration from the book and add their personal inspirations to it! This book may become their own journey journal—and one of the many mementos the girls will cherish through their years in Girl Scouting and beyond!

A Smorgasbord of Sisterhood!

smor gas bord *(noun)*
an extensive array or variety

Variety is the spice of life. It's also the spice of sisterhood—and Girl Scout leadership journeys! Throughout the sessions, Seniors see how diversifying their friendship and sisterhood circles adds richness to their lives and their ability to take action in the world.

And, built into every Sample Session, is an extensive array of confidence-boosting, creative activities to develop girls leadership skills, including:

1. Visual Arts
Right away, in Session 1, the girls team up to create a visual Sisterhood Smorgasbord, a fun, free-form representation of what sisterhood means to them as a way of defining sisterhood for themselves and starting their sisterhood story. They can hang it at each journey gathering as a symbol of their sisterhood, and add to it or change it as their views evolve along the journey.

2. Performing Arts
Girls get to try their hands at playwriting to share how sisterhood has shaped their stories. Then they can go all out and perform their creations, too.

3. Culinary Arts
Girls have fun making and enjoying a range of foods, from a smorgasbord of healthful snacks to a sweet watermelon and mango salsa to tea and sandwiches, showing that sharing food can be artful and sisterly, too.

Sisterly extras for the journey!

Buddy Button Bracelets fashioned from buttons the girls exchange can serve as symbols of the close connections they share with friends and sisters.

Sisterhood Thank-You Notes These paper-doll thank-you notes, made from vintage wallpaper, wrapping paper, or newsprint, offer a sisterhood of appreciation.

The girls might also consider enjoying some of the creative projects in their journey book together with the full team:

Friendship key chains or pendants made from two matching pieces of an old jigsaw puzzle remind girls of their connection to one another (page 42, girls book).

Friendship potpourri made from a base of yellow roses (known as the friendship rose), as well as spices and other ingredients, demonstrate that a diversity of ingredients (in sisterhood and potpourri!) makes life more beautiful and interesting (page 14, girls' book).

STORIES + CREATIVITY

Why Self-Esteem Matters!

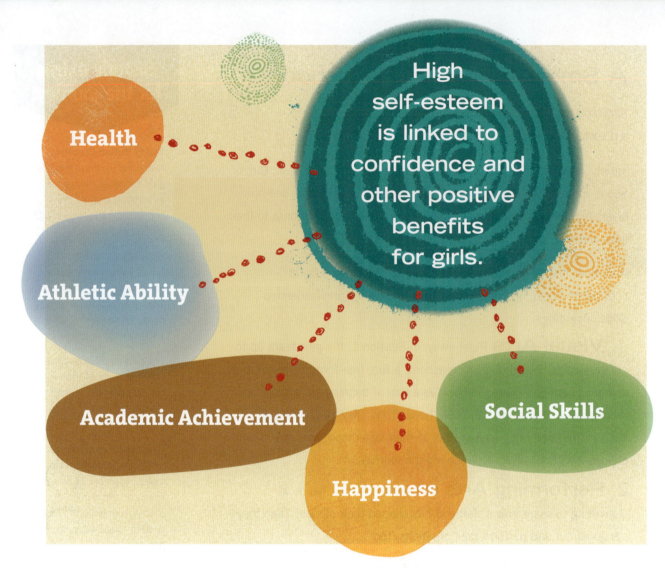

Self-esteem means how a girl feels about herself—her abilities, her body, her capacity to seek and meet challenges in the world. Supporting and strengthening Seniors' self-esteem are goals of this journey. With strong self-esteem, girls are likely to avoid any drop in confidence as they move through adolescence. Instead their confidence will soar!

Session Plans Make the Most of Seniors' Skills

The Sample Session plans starting on page 28 offer opportunities for the girls to enhance their skills and develop new ones while taking into account the abilities and needs of Senior-age girls. When planning additional creative adventures, keep in mind that ninth- and 10th-graders:

Are beginning to clarify their own values, consider alternative points of view on controversial issues, and see multiple aspects of a situation.	*So ask them to explain the reasoning behind their decisions. Engage girls in role-play and performances where others can watch on, and offer alternatives to a process or solution.*
Have strong problem-solving and critical thinking skills, and can plan and reflect on their learning experiences.	*So they are more than able to develop projects that will create sustainable solutions in their communities. Be sure to have girls plan and follow up on these experiences through creative and discussion-based reflective activities.*
Spend more time with peers than with their families and are very concerned about friends and relationships with others their age.	*So they'll enjoy teaming up for activities and Take Action Projects, especially ones that tackle relationship issues. Follow this journey's theme and alter the makeup of the groups with each activity so girls interact with those they might not usually team-up with.*
Frequently enjoy expressing their individuality.	*So encourage them to do so in their dress, creative expression, and thinking. And assist them in devising news ways to express their individuality.*
Feel they have lots of responsibilities and pressures—from home, school, peers, work, etc.	*So acknowledge these pressures and share with the girls how stress can limit health, creativity, and productivity. Help them release stress in creative ways.*
Are continuing to navigate their increasing independence and expectations from adults.	*So trust them to plan and make key decisions, allow them to experience "fun failure," and learn from trying something new and making mistakes.*

Promoting Well-Being Along the Journey

Girl Scouting is guided by a positive philosophy of inclusion that benefits all. On this journey especially, it is hoped that girls will increase their feelings of being powerful, capable, and strong as they enhance their skills and develop new ones. So, as the Girl Scout Law says, "be a sister to every Girl Scout." Determine whether any girls are new to town, have a disability, don't speak English as a first language, or have parents getting a divorce. Often what counts most is being open-minded and aware, staying flexible, and creatively varying your approach with the girls.

The Sisterhood Award

WHERE MIGHT GIRLS FIND A SISTERHOOD ISSUE?

The best place to look for a sisterhood issue is in a sisterhood. The girls might start with their Girl Scout council and then check out the larger sisterhood of the World Organization of Girl Guides and Girl Scouts (WAGGGS). On the WAGGGS Web site (wagggsworld.org/en/issues/take_action), they can find ways Girl Scouts and Girl Guides are taking action on a global scale.

Also, the sample Sisterhood Projects throughout the girls' book suggest sisterhood issues to tackle. They also step the girls through how to plan a Sisterhood Project that will have positive impact:

- Finding the Beauty in Images of Beauty, p. 20
- Call Out That Inner Beauty, p. 32
- Friendship Mentorship, p 43
- Friendship Mixer p. 56

But the sample projects are just that—samples. Encourage the girls to use their creativity to find their own by asking around: *What issues are women and girls passionate about in their community?*

On this journey, Seniors have the opportunity to earn the Sisterhood Award, a leadership award that has them exploring the three keys: Discover, Connect, and Take Action! To earn the award, the girls define a sisterhood issue, create a plan for how to Take Action on that issue, and then Take Action!

The Sisterhood Award

What it means for Seniors: Girls understand the power of sisterhood in their own lives and in the world.

As with all leadership awards earned on Girl Scout journeys, the Sisterhood Award gives girls the planing, teamwork, and networking skills they need to pursue the Girl Scout Gold Award, the highest award in the Girl Scouts. The steps to the Sisterhood Award are listed below and detailed on pages 68–73 of the girls' book. You'll find a Sisterhood Award icon throughout the Sessions plans to indicate those journey activities that move girls toward the award.

STEPS TO THE SISTERHOOD AWARD

1. Define a Sisterhood Issue for Yourself
2. Develop Your Mission!
3. Make the Big Decisions!
4. Logistics Time!
5. Creating the Project Timeline

No matter what issue the girls tackle, keep in mind that a great Sisterhood Project gives them the opportunity to:

- find and think about a sisterhood issue they've never thought about before
- figure out what they can do about a sisterhood issue they care about
- meet and talk to new people (and that expands their sisterhood!)
- understand how to focus efforts, so they get results despite obstacles
- start some change that keeps on going even after they're done
- step back and say, "I made this change happen!"
- be a true example of sisterhood in action!

LADDER OF LEADERSHIP

As Girl Scouts take journeys and earn the awards, they're climbing a ladder that lets them be leaders in their own lives and in the world! Pass it on!

It's Your World— Change It!

Ambassadors raise their voices to advocate for issues they care about.

Seniors learn that leaders have a vision and can move the world a step closer to it.

Cadettes develop the people skills that leaders need.

Juniors learn that leaders need power—their own, their team's, and their community's.

 Brownies go on a quest to find the three keys to leadership.

 Daisies have fun—and learn leadership skills—in the garden.

It's Your Story— Tell It!

Girls move dreams forward!

AMBASSADOR

 Girls see how much sisterhood does for the world!

SENIOR

Girls put the ME in media.

CADETTE

Girls explore all the roles open to them in life.

JUNIOR

 Girls explore their place in the wide world of girls.

BROWNIE

 Girls learn they can care for animals and themselves.

DAISY

It's Your Planet— Love It!

 Ambassadors learn that leaders aim for justice.

 Seniors find out what leaders can sow for Earth.

 Cadettes become leaders in clearing the air!

 Juniors bring energy solutions to the world.

 Brownies take the lead in saving Earth's water.

 Daisies learn to protect Earth's treasures.

What You'll Find in Each Sample Session Plan

THE JOURNEY SNAPSHOT gives an overview of what's ahead.

Journey activities are sequenced to give girls lots of fun and exciting challenges centered around earning the journey's three leadership awards. But don't feel you and the girls must do everything in the Sample Sessions or in the order given. Think of journey activities as pieces that can be mixed, matched, and coordinated according to the needs of your group of Seniors.

AT A GLANCE gives the session's goal, activities, and recommended materials.

TOWARD THE AWARD ICONS indicate activities that step girls toward a leadership award.

CEREMONIES, opening and closing, mark the Seniors' time together.

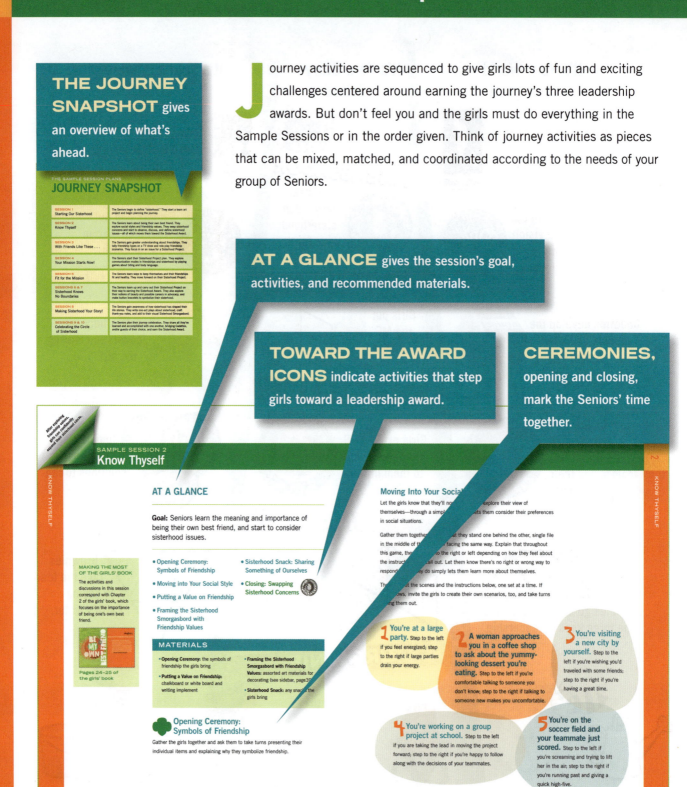

WHAT YOU'LL FIND IN EACH SAMPLE SESSION PLAN

CREATIVE ACTIVITIES encourage self-expression and teamwork on the sisterhood theme.

WHAT TO SAY A full script for you to use! Must you follow it? No! Let it guide you, but be yourself!

PROJECT PLANNERS give girls tips and advice, and space to step out their project.

SNACKS offer girls healthful treats they can make and enjoy.

15

Creating a Network of Journey Resources

GO ONLINE FOR LETTERS HOME

Visit the Journeys section of girlscouts.org for suggestions on how to start your Friends and Family Network and keep its members informed and motivated to join in all the fun the Seniors will have on this journey! You'll find:

- Ideas for reaching out to local experts and other resources
- Checklist for Friends and Family Network

You'll get a break and expand the girls' awareness of community by asking family members, friends, and friends of friends to support and enhance the Seniors' gatherings. So go ahead and "hand off" activities and prep steps to a Friends and Family Network. Here are some tips:

- Before the journey begins, aim for a brief get-together (even online!) with the girls, their parents, caregivers, relatives, and friends.

- Find out who likes to do what, identify assistants for various activities, and see who has time for behind-the-scenes preparations, gathering supplies, and project support.

- Keep in mind that in some families, an aunt, older sibling, cousin, or other adult may be most able to participate.

More Print and Online Journey Resources

- ☐ *Girl Scout Safety Activity Checkpoints* detail the safety net provided for girls in Girl Scouting. Seek them out from your council and keep them handy!

- ☐ **Journey maps, in the Journeys section of girlscouts.org,** show you and the girls how to mix the outdoors, trips, badges, and Girl Scout traditions (including cookies!) into your journey fun.

- ☐ *It's Your Journey—Customize It!* is your guide to making the most of Girl Scout leadership journeys.

- ☐ *Volunteer Essentials* is your guide to all things Girl Scouts! Seek it out from your council.

- ☐ **Online activities** for girls to enjoy on their own, with friends, and with their Senior group, are at www.girlscouts.org/itsyourstory.

Mission: Sisterhood

SENIOR JOURNEY PEOPLE POWER

FRIENDS & FAMILY NETWORK: Name	Willing to help with:	Phone and e-mail address

COUNCIL CONTACTS: Name	Willing to help with:	Phone and e-mail address

LOCAL EXPERTS: Name	Area of expertise	Phone and e-mail address

Girl Scout Traditions and Ceremonies

GIRL SCOUTS!

As Girls Scouts celebrates its 100th anniversary in 2012, this leadership journey is a reminder of the long-cherished Girl Scout tradition of girls creating change in their local and global communities. "It's Your Story—Tell It" continues to tell the story of Girl Scouting—a story of leadership and making the world a better place.

GIRL SCOUT DAYS TO CELEBRATE

- **Founder's Day**
  October 31
  Juliette "Daisy" Gordon Low's birthday

- **World Thinking Day**
  February 22
  A day for Girl Scouts and Girl Guides throughout the world to think about one another

- **Girl Scout Birthday**
  March 12
  The day in 1912 when Juliette Gordon Low officially registered the organization's first 18 girl members in Savannah, Georgia

Even the briefest of ceremonies can take girls away from the everyday to think about hopes, intentions, commitments, and feelings. A ceremony marks a separation from whatever girls have just come from (school, work, dance class, math club) and creates the sense that what will happen now is special and important. So, find out how and when girls want ceremonies.

Girl Scout ceremonies can be as simple as gathering in a circle, lighting a candle, and sharing one hope—or reflecting together on one line of the Girl Scout Law. Or girls might read poems, play music, or sing songs. Invite them to create their own ways to mark their time together as special.

Sharing food, recipes, and meals is a long-standing tradition in Girl Scouts. This journey offers many suggestions for sharing food in sisterly ways. The Seniors might enjoy these traditions, too:

QUIET SIGN

The Quiet Sign is a way to silence a crowd without shouting at anyone. The sign is made by holding up the right hand with all five fingers extended. It refers to the original Fifth Law of Girl Scouting: A Girl Scout is courteous.

SWAPS

Trading SWAPS ("Special Whatchamacallits Affectionately Pinned Somewhere") is a Girl Scout tradition for exchanging small keepsakes. It started long ago when Girl Scouts and Girl Guides from England first gathered for fun, song, and making new friends. Swaps are still a fun way to meet and promote friendship. Each swap offers a memory of a special event or a particular girl—it usually says something about a Girl Scout's group or highlights something special about where she lives. And it's simple; it could be made from donated or recycled goods.

TRAVEL

Travel, whether national or local, is a big part of Girl Scouting. Encourage the girls to check out the *destinations* program of travel opportunities at girlscouts.org. For international travel, the World Association of Girl Guides and Girl Scouts (WAGGGS) offers a wealth of opportunities. This umbrella organization for our worldwide sisterhood, founded in 1928, advocates globally on issues of importance to girls and young women. For WAGGGS, as for GSUSA, advocacy means "speaking, doing, and educating." Visits to the four World Centers operated by WAGGGS are highly popular international travel destinations for Girl Scouts. The girls can learn more by searching on "world centers" at girlscouts.org.

GIRL SCOUT GOLD AWARD

Earning the Girl Scout Gold Award is an important tradition in Girl Scouting—and a great way to demonstrate leadership. While on leadership journeys (like this one), girls learn to use the three keys to leadership: Discover, Connect, and Take Action. And they gain the valuable planning, networking, and teamwork skills they need to go on to earn the Girl Scout Gold Award.

Encourage the Seniors to read about the award and girls who have earned it at girlscouts.org. They might ask their council to put them in touch with some of the young women from their region who've earned this highest award in Girl Scouting.

Keys to Girl Leadership

Girl Scouting prepares girls to be leaders—in their own daily lives and in the world around them. We do this through the Girl Scout Leadership Experience, pictured below, which is the basis for everything girls do in Girl Scouting. The three keys to leadership—Discover (self), Connect (team up and network with others), and Take Action (make a difference in the world)—are a shorthand way of capturing all 15 of the national leadership benefits girls get in Girl Scouting.

As you can see in the charts on pages 86–88, all of the experiences in this journey have been created to engage girls in exploring these three keys to leadership. In fact, that's what makes a Girl Scout journey so special: Everything girls and their adult guides need to explore the leadership keys is built right in! So all along the way, you will be guiding the Seniors toward leadership skills and qualities they can use right now—and all their lives. Keep in mind that the intended benefits to girls are the cumulative result of traveling through an entire journey—and everything else girls experience in Girl Scouting!

How Girls Have Fun in Girl Scouts

In Girl Scouting, girls enjoy activities based on the three keys to leadership and built on three processes that make Girl Scouting distinct from school and other extracurricular activities. The keys and processes are built right into the journey for you—in the Sample Session plans! So you know a little more about how the processes play out for Seniors, here's a quick summary:

Girl Led means girls play an active part in figuring out the what, where, when, how, and why of their activities. Encourage them to lead the planning, decision-making, learning, and fun as much as possible. This ensures that girls experience leadership opportunities as they prepare to become active participants in their communities. With Seniors, you could:

- guide and act as a resource for girls as they plan complex projects
- encourage girls to question/investigate things they take for granted
- encourage girls to share what excites them along the journey with younger girls, peers, and family in a way that allows them to educate and inspire

Learning by Doing engages girls in continuous cycles of action and reflection that result in deeper understanding of concepts and mastery of practical skills. As girls participate in activities and then reflect on them, they discover their own answers, gain new skills, and share ideas. It's important for girls to connect their experiences to their lives. With Seniors, you could:

- act as a resource as they plan their own learning experiences
- expose girls to multiple perspectives and resources for problem-solving
- encourage documentation of their learning, reflection, and planning

Cooperative Learning has girls work together toward goals with mutual respect and collaboration. Working together in all-girl environments encourages girls to feel powerful and emotionally and physically safe, and allows them to experience a sense of belonging. With Seniors, you could:

- promote participation in projects that reach beyond familiar communities
- guide them to see connections between individual action and global solutions
- expose girls to multiple ways of learning together (experts, films, etc.)

KEEP IT GIRL LED

One of the greatest benefits of Girl Scouting is that girls of all ages have the opportunity to take the lead in ways they don't at school, at home, or in other places in their lives.

So get this journey off to the right start by encouraging the girls to take the lead from the get-go. Let them know you are a supporting resource and their biggest cheerleader but they are the ones who choose, direct, and lead their journey experiences. Then sit back and feel proud as you watch the girls confidently take the reins in Girl Scouts and beyond.

IT'S NOT ALL ABOUT DOING

Girls need time to talk between the action, so they can capture what their experiences have taught them and keep on growing! That's why you'll see discussion starters and suggested questions you can use with the girls in every sample session.

SAVOR THE TEAMWORK!

Girls not only benefit from working in teams, but from speaking openly and often about how their teamwork is going and how they use relationship strategies purposefully to achieve the best results in teamwork and in life.

What It All Means for Girls

All activities in this leadership journey relate to Discovering, Connecting, and Taking Action—the three Girl Scout keys to leadership! Plus, Girl Led, Cooperative Learning, and Learning By Doing processes make the activities fun and powerful for girls. Here, in an activity from Session 1, you can see how these processes and the national Girl Scout outcomes—the benefits we want for girls—play out during a team gathering. Throughout Mission: Sisterhood, you'll see processes and outcomes play out again and again. Before you know it, you'll be sharing these valuable aspects of Girl Scouting through whatever Seniors do!

This journey is **Girl Led** from the very start: Girls think about and begin to define "sisterhood" for themselves in Session 1. By having the girls collaborate on this creative project to define "sisterhood" instead of only sharing in a discussion, the girls are engaged in both the **Learning by Doing** and **Cooperative Learning** processes. And here, they are also learning about how to represent their shared definition, strengthening their teamwork abilities, and advancing toward the **Connect outcome, Girls promote cooperation and team building**.

FROM SAMPLE SESSION 1

Starting Our Sisterhood Story: Creating a Visual Smorgasbord

Gather the girls together and welcome them to this journey all about sisterhood by saying something like:

- *Sisterhood . . . what does this word really mean to any of us?*

- *Most of you probably know that the Girl Scout Promise asks us to "be a sister to every Girl Scout."*

- *But how often do we really think about what that means?*

- *Does it mean something different to you now than it did years earlier, when you might have been a Girl Scout Brownie?*

- *Before any of us answers these questions individually, let's create a shared answer—by getting creative together!*

Point the girls to the large roll of paper and the stacks of pictures of women and girls you and your Network have gathered, and say:

- *Go ahead and dive into these piles and use these images, whole or cut up, to create a visual record of what sisterhood means to all of you!*

- *You can attach your images to the roll of paper any way you want, adding drawings, words, or any decorative elements you like from the art materials on hand.*

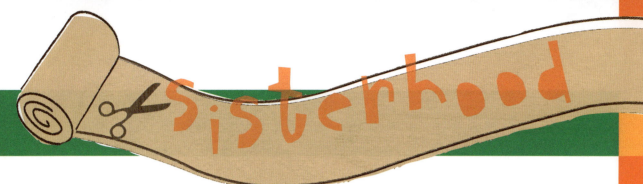

- *Don't think of this as a simple collage but as something much richer and deeper: a visual Sisterhood Smorgasbord!*
- *The important thing is to work as a team and talk out what you want to do as it is happening. This is your Sisterhood Smorgasbord, so create it as a sisterhood!*
- *When you're ready, we'll all take a look at what this smorgasbord says about us and our understanding of sisterhood!*

The girls may need 30 minutes or longer to get the smorgasbord going. When they're satisfied with it, ask the girls to take note of any themes (see suggestions at right) running through it.

Then get the girls talking about what sisterhood means to them, based on their smorgasbord, with questions like these (or others that come to mind based on themes they see in their creative work):

- *What were you were aiming for in this smorgasbord? What sort of vision did you start with?*
- *How did you decide what images to include and where to place them?*
- *What made you want to cut up some images but not others?*
- *You've grouped many women together but left a few on their own. Why?*
- *Why did you add decorations to this part of the smorgasbord but not that?*

As the girls answer, guide them to see that they've started to create a visual representation of their definition of sisterhood, and they are now talking out that definition, too.

Let them know that their understanding of sisterhood will grow and evolve on this *MISSION: SISTERHOOD!* journey. You might say: Expanding your understanding of sisterhood and all it can do for you and the world is what this leadership experience is all about!

Then transition the discussion to how, in creating this Sisterhood Smorgasbord, they *formed a sisterhood!* Ask:

- *Did you decide as a team who would do what on this collaborative effort, or did you just get started based on individual interests and talents?*

> With these questions, the Seniors get to analyze the choices they made in developing their Visual Smorgasbord and look for themes that may exist in their creative work, all while helping them achieve the **Discover Outcome, Girls develop critical thinking**.

> This notion of the benefits of expanding one's sisterhood is central to the journey. It not only helps **girls develop healthy relationships (Discover Outcome)**, but also aids girls in **feeling connected to their communities locally and globally (a Connect Outcome)**.

WHAT IT ALL MEANS FOR GIRLS

WHAT IT ALL MEANS FOR GIRLS

Both the Cooperative Learning and **Learning by Doing** processes are reinforced by these discussion questions that ask the girls to reflect on how they worked together on this creative piece. Understanding how they work as a team will help the Seniors throughout the journey as they expand their Sisterhood Network, and continue to progress towards **Connect Outcome, Girls promote Cooperation and Team Building**.

WHAT THEMES TO LOOK FOR IN THE SISTERHOOD SMORGASBORD?

- Are there more women than girls, or more girls than women?

- Are images collaged together to show women and/or girls teaming up in various ways?

- How diverse are the women and girls?

- Are there patterns to the colors in the smorgasbord?

- To the sizes and shapes of images?

- The decorative additions?

- *What challenges, if any, did you face in creating this together?*

- *Is this smorgasbord the result of a shared vision? Or did one or a few of you lead this vision?*

- *Now that you look at the smorgasbord as a whole, is it a vision all of you are comfortable calling your own?*

Guide the girls to see that there are many ways they could have come at this project effectively—and no one right way. You might say:

- *Teaming up in a way that best fits the task at hand, while taking into account everyone's talents and strengths: That's what sisterhood is all about, and that's what leadership is about, too. This way of teaming up is usually the best way to accomplish a group goal creatively and well.*

- *All along this journey, you'll have opportunities to team up to create important change. So how we work together as a sisterhood is at the heart of this journey. And the sisterhood we develop will help shape your story, too!*

Then suggest that the girls hang their Sisterhood Smorgasbord at each journey gathering as a symbolic reminder of all that sisterhood means to them. Encourage them to update the smorgasbord at any time, as their views of sisterhood expand and evolve along the journey. Ask them to think of this smorgasbord as a story that will continue all along their journey.

Ask them to also take time, on their own, to look back over the first pages of their book to answer these question: *How do you feel about the definition of sisterhood that is given? Does it make sense? How well does it match up with what you and your sister Seniors have just created in the Sisterhood Smorgasbord?*

Again, when girls pay close attention to the themes of their collaborative Sisterhood Smorgasbord, they are examining their own and others' views of sisterhood and the world which helps them both **develop their critical thinking skills (Discover Outcome)** and also consider how they **advance issues of diversity in a multicultural world (Connect Outcome)** with this and other future projects.

Your Perspective on Leadership

The Girl Scout leadership keys—Discover + Connect + Take Action—demonstrate that leadership happens from the inside out. Your thoughts, enthusiasm, and approach will influence the Seniors, so take a few minutes now—and throughout the journey—to apply the three "keys" of leadership to yourself.

Discover + Connect + Take Action = Leadership

DISCOVER This journey is about the Seniors feeling confident and powerful about how sisterhood plays out in their life and in the world. How does sisterhood make you feel most confident?

_____
_____
_____

CONNECT Who would you like to add to your community network in order to make this journey an enriching experience for you and the Seniors? Why do you think it's important for Seniors to meet new people and begin to expand their community network?

_____
_____
_____

TAKE ACTION How does your role as a volunteer with Girl Scout Seniors contribute to making the world better? In what ways do you believe Senior-age girls can use sisterhood to educate and inspire others to make the world a better place?

_____
_____

Every session in this journey has been created to help girls become **confident leaders—** in their own lives and in the world!

How?

The journey gets girls using the **3 keys to leadership: Discover, Connect,** and **Take Action.**

Girls **Discover** themselves.

They **Connect** with others.

And they **Take Action** in the world!

And in every session of the journey, **girls lead, team up, and learn by doing.** (And you'll learn right along with them. Have a wonderful journey!)

For more on the leadership keys and Girl Scout processes and their benefits to girls, see pages 20–21 and 86–88 in this guide, and *Transforming Leadership: Focusing on Outcomes of the New Girl Scout Leadership Experience* (GSUSA, 2008) and *Transforming Leadership Continued* (GSUSA, 2009). Both publications are available on girlscouts.org.

THE SAMPLE SESSION PLANS
JOURNEY SNAPSHOT

SESSION 1 Starting Our Sisterhood	The Seniors begin to define "sisterhood." They start a team art project and begin planning the journey.
SESSION 2 Know Thyself	The Seniors learn about being their own best friend. They explore social styles and friendship values. They swap sisterhood concerns and start to observe, discuss, and define sisterhood issues—all of which moves them toward the Sisterhood Award.
SESSION 3 With Friends Like These . . .	The Seniors gain greater understanding about friendships. They tally friendship types on a TV show and role-play friendship scenarios. They focus in on an issue for a Sisterhood Project.
SESSION 4 Your Mission Starts Now!	The Seniors start their Sisterhood Project plan. They explore communication modes in friendships and sisterhood by playing games about txting and body language.
SESSION 5 Fit for the Mission	The Seniors learn ways to keep themselves and their friendships fit and healthy. They move forward on their Sisterhood Project.
SESSIONS 6 & 7 Sisterhood Knows No Boundaries	The Seniors team up and carry out their Sisterhood Project on their way to earning the Sisterhood Award. They also explore their notions of beauty and possible careers in advocacy, and make button bracelets to symbolize their sisterhood.
SESSION 8 Making Sisterhood Your Story!	The Seniors gain awareness of how sisterhood has shaped their life stories. They write one-act plays about sisterhood, craft thank-you notes, and add to their visual Sisterhood Smorgasbord.
SESSIONS 9 & 10 Celebrating the Circle of Sisterhood	The Seniors plan their journey celebration. They share all they've learned and accomplished with one another, bridging Cadettes, and/or guests of their choice, and earn the Sisterhood Award.

This journey kicks off with a rock-solid base of confidence: the power of girls together!

SAMPLE SESSION 1
Starting Our Sisterhood

MAKING THE MOST OF THE GIRLS' BOOK

Each Sample Session in this journey relates to various parts of the girls' book. In this session, for example, you can refer the girls to the introduction on page 5 of their book, which defines sisterhood. This definition relates to both the "Starting Our Sisterhood Story" activity and the Closing Ceremony. See page 29 of this guide for more on how to make use of this sisterhood definition with the girls.

"Customizing the Journey and the Sisterhood Award" relates directly to page 8 of the girls' book, where the steps to the award are given generally, and pages 68–77, where the steps are detailed.

Pages 68–69, girls' book

AT A GLANCE

Goal: Seniors begin to define "sisterhood" for themselves and their team.

- Starting Our Sisterhood Story: Creating a Visual Smorgasbord
- Sisterhood Snack: The Smorgasbord
- Customizing the Journey and the Sisterhood Award
- Closing Ceremony: Sisterhood Is . . .

MATERIALS

- **Starting Our Sisterhood Story:** large roll of paper; diverse images of women and girls, famous or anonymous, active or not (from newspapers, varied magazines—not just fashion!—books, the Web, or anything that can be cut up and attached to the roll of paper); glue, tape, staples, or other adhesives; assorted decorations (glitter, stars, sequins, ribbon, tissue paper, etc.); markers

  Sisterhood Snack: any simple, healthful snacks your Network has provided for this first gathering

  Closing Ceremony: sheet of paper; pens or markers

PREPARE AHEAD

- Reach out to the girls in your group and your Network for a wide variety of pictures of women and girls for "Starting Our Sisterhood Story" (see Materials list above). Aim for varied, active scenes and enough images to create multiple piles.

- Also ask the Network to help create a smorgasbord of simple, healthful snacks for this first gathering.

- On the day of this session, hang the roll of paper or lay it out on a large table so girls can add images and decorations to it.

GET CREATIVE

Starting Our Sisterhood Story: Creating a Visual Smorgasbord

Gather the girls together and welcome them to this journey all about sisterhood by saying something like:

- *Sisterhood . . . what does this word really mean to any of us?*
- *Most of you probably know that the Girl Scout Promise asks us to "be a sister to every Girl Scout."*
- *But how often do we really think about what that means?*
- *Does it mean something different to you now than it did years earlier, when you might have been a Girl Scout Brownie?*
- *Before any of us answers these questions individually, let's create a shared answer—by getting creative together!*

Point the girls to the large roll of paper and the stacks of pictures of women and girls you and your Network have gathered, and say:

- *Go ahead and dive into these piles and use these images, whole or cut up, to create a visual record of what sisterhood means to all of you!*
- *You can attach your images to the roll of paper any way you want, adding drawings, words, or any decorative elements you like from the art materials on hand.*
- *Don't think of this as a simple collage but as something much richer and deeper: a visual Sisterhood Smorgasbord!*
- *The important thing is to work as a team and talk out what you want to do as it is happening. This is your Sisterhood Smorgasbord, so create it as a sisterhood!*
- *When you're ready, we'll all take a look at what this smorgasbord says about us and our understanding of sisterhood!*

SO WHAT IS SISTERHOOD, ANYWAY?

Sisterhood, as the opening page of the girls' book points out, is found in those special moments of connection experienced with girlfriends, mothers, sisters, aunts, and female cousins. Sisterhood is also all the moments the Seniors will experience with all the girls and women they have yet—to meet!

Sisterhood is so much a part of the Seniors' lives, and their stories. Sisterhood moments help them see who they are and their place in the world. Sisterhood expands their sense of themselves and gives them the power to create their own life story.

The hope is that on this journey, as the Seniors' stories grow, they can also better grow the story for all women and girls.

1

STARTING OUR SISTERHOOD

WHAT THEMES TO LOOK FOR IN THE SISTERHOOD SMORGASBORD?

- Are there more women than girls, or more girls than women?
- Are images collaged together to show women and/or girls teaming up in various ways?
- How diverse are the women and girls?
- Are there patterns to the colors in the smorgasbord?
- To the sizes and shapes of images?
- The decorative additions?

The girls may need 30 minutes or longer to get the smorgasbord going. When they're satisfied with it, ask the girls to take note of any themes (see suggestions at left) running through it.

Then get the girls talking about what sisterhood means to them, based on their smorgasbord, with questions like these (or others that come to mind based on themes they see in their creative work):

- *What were you were aiming for in this smorgasbord? What sort of vision did you start with?*
- *How did you decide what images to include and where to place them?*
- *What made you want to cut up some images but not others?*
- *You've grouped many women together but left a few on their own. Why?*
- *Why did you add decorations to this part of the smorgasbord but not that?*

As the girls answer, guide them to see that they've started to create a visual representation of their definition of sisterhood, and they are now talking out that definition, too.

Let them know that their understanding of sisterhood will grow and evolve on this *MISSION: SISTERHOOD!* journey. You might say: *Expanding your understanding of sisterhood and all it can do for you and the world is what this leadership experience is all about!*

Then transition the discussion to how, in creating this Sisterhood Smorgasbord, they *formed a sisterhood!* Ask:

- *Did you decide as a team who would do what on this collaborative effort, or did you just get started based on individual interests and talents?*

- What challenges, if any, did you face in creating this together?
- Is this smorgasbord a result of a shared vision? Or did one or a few of you lead this vision?
- Now that you look at the smorgasbord as a whole, is it a vision all of you are comfortable calling your own?

Guide the girls to see that there are many ways they could have come at this project effectively—and no one right way. You might say:

- Teaming up in a way that best fits the task at hand, while taking into account everyone's talents and strengths: That's what sisterhood is all about, and that's what leadership is about, too. This way of teaming up is usually the best way to accomplish a group goal creatively and well.
- All along this journey, you'll have opportunities to team up to create important change. So how we work together as a sisterhood is at the heart of this journey. And the sisterhood we develop will help shape your story, too!

Then suggest that the girls hang their Sisterhood Smorgasbord at each journey gathering as a symbolic reminder of all that sisterhood means to them. Encourage them to update the smorgasbord at any time, as their views of sisterhood expand and evolve along the journey. Ask them to think of this smorgasbord as a story that will continue all along their journey.

Ask them to also take time, on their own, to look back over the first pages of their book to answer these questions: *How do you feel about the definition of sisterhood that is given? Does it make sense? How well does it match up with what you and your sister Seniors just created in the Sisterhood Smorgasbord?*

SISTERHOOD SNACK: THE SMORGASBORD

Serve the smorgasbord of healthful snacks that you and your Network have assembled. You might say to the Seniors: *A sisterhood supports its members in many ways. One way is supporting one another in being healthy, and that includes eating healthful foods like the ones in this smorgasbord.*

STARTING OUR SISTERHOOD

1

CONFIDENCE TO GO FOR THE GOLD!

Earning the Sisterhood Award will give Seniors the planning skills and experience they need to carry out a Gold Award project that moves them to the top of the Girl Scout leadership ladder! But the *real* award will be the confidence they gain in the process! Find more details about the Gold Award online at girlscouts.org.

Page 9, girls' book

AT A GLANCE

Goal: Seniors begin to define "sisterhood" for themselves and their team.

- **Starting Our Sisterhood Story: Creating a Visual Smorgasbord**
- **Sisterhood Snack: The Smorgasbord**
- **Customizing the Journey and the Sisterhood Award**
- **Closing Ceremony: Sisterhood Is . . .**

STRETCH THAT SISTERHOOD!

Encourage the Seniors to plan some "sisterhood time" that stretches them toward new, physical challenges. They might opt for a day at a rock-climbing wall, sculling on a river or lake, or a weekend campout. Or maybe their team can link with other Senior groups on *MISSION: SISTERHOOD!* and plan a campout together.

chat time!

Give the girls time to think about how they want to plan and schedule their journey, using the "Make It Your Own!" planner pages in this guide (pages 34–35. They don't need to decide everything today; they can keep planning all along the way. Ask them to consider these basics:

- ☐ How much time do they have for the journey?
- ☐ What kind of add-ons might they like: trips, outdoor activities, guest speakers?
- ☐ Do they want to create their own healthful snacks for each gathering? Should the snacks take the form of a potluck at times?

Closing Ceremony: Sisterhood Is . . .

Gather the girls together and hold up a sheet of paper with the words "Sisterhood is . . ." written across the top. Ask the girls to take turns passing the paper so that each can write one line on it that completes the sentence. Say something like:

- *Write whatever comes to mind—the first thing that pops into your head. Keep it short!*
- *Once you've written your statement, fold the paper over (so your writing is concealed) and pass it to the next girl so she can write her sentence.*
- *When we've all written our sentences, we're going to unfold the paper and read what we wrote, like one long sisterhood poem.*

Looking Ahead to Session 2

Ask the girls to bring an item that they think symbolizes friendship to their next gathering. You might offer some examples, such as:

- a friendship bracelet to represent bonding.
- song lyrics that represent a "true" friendship, or even a bad one.
- a yellow rose, considered a friendship flower.
- a Band-Aid to represent helping.
- a hair clip or other personal accessory to acknowledge a friend with a great sense of style.

Since these are symbolic items, they don't need to be personal. For example, instead of bringing a photograph of friends, a Senior might simply bring a picture frame. Either way, this is simply a show-and-tell activity; the objects will go home with the girls at the end of the Session.

Also, since the Seniors' next gathering is all about getting to know themselves better, ask them to bring a favorite, easy-to-eat, sharable "Sisterhood Snack."

WHAT'S REQUIRED? JOY, JOY, JOY!

One of the best things about a sisterhood is the fun it can bring to girls' lives. Although some serious topics are explored on this journey, laughter will be heard all along the way! Encourage the girls to experience the joy of sisterhood in as many ways as possible. Here are some ideas to get them started:

• Have a dance break: The girls might like to make a play list of friendship songs and use it to take 15-minute dance breaks throughout the journey.

• Have a sister-themed viewing night (see page 45) to watch films like "Sister Act" or old TV shows, such as "Laverne & Shirley" and "The Golden Girls."

• Have a Sisterhood Supper Club by scheduling three potluck dinners throughout the journey.

• Have an old-fashioned slumber party—don't forget the popcorn!

Mission: Sisterhood!

MISSION: SISTERHOOD! Make It Your Own!

THINK ABOUT . . .	WHAT WE'LL DO
THE SISTERHOOD AWARD: Are you interested in earning the award? What do you hope to learn and explore by doing so? Do you want to complete the award steps as individuals and discuss and share insights with the team? Or progress through the steps in teams, or even as one big team? Would you like to use your gatherings primarily to work on the award, or devote time to other activities as well?	
FREESTYLING: Perhaps you or other team members (or all of you, in turn!) would like to lead the explorations and discussions at various gatherings. You could tailor, tweak, and make them your own as you go. Find out which team members might like to "sign on" to lead.	
NETWORKING FOR SISTERHOOD: What might you like to learn from other women and girls in your community? Who might you like to invite to one or more of the Senior gatherings?	
CREATIVITY: What artists might you like to meet? What creative mediums might you like to explore? How might you further your creativity along this journey?	

Mission: Sisterhood!

THINK ABOUT . . .	WHAT WE'LL DO
CEREMONIES: What might you like to do to mark the opening and/or closing of your time together as special and apart from all the busyness of your daily life? Would you like to share a good thing and a challenge you've experienced in life between Senior meetings? How will your team share leadership? What values will you share with one another?	
SKILL BUILDING: What leadership skills might you like to improve upon on this journey? What skills can you share with your sister Seniors?	
CAREER EXPLORATIONS: Whom might you like to meet? What sisterhood-related careers are you interested in hearing about?	
SISTERHOOD AND THE GREAT OUTDOORS: How would you like to spend some time connecting to nature? Day hikes? A weekend camping retreat? Trying out new activities where sisterhood can blossom? Linking up with other Senior groups for a mega-campout with time to share ideas and sisterhood stories?	

After exploring friendship values, girls can confidently expand their sisterhood circle.

SAMPLE SESSION 2
Know Thyself

AT A GLANCE

Goal: Seniors learn the meaning and importance of being their own best friend, and start to consider sisterhood issues.

- **Opening Ceremony: Symbols of Friendship**
- **Moving into Your Social Style**
- **Putting a Value on Friendship**
- **Framing the Sisterhood Smorgasbord with Friendship Values**
- **Sisterhood Snack: Sharing Something of Ourselves**
- **Closing: Swapping Sisterhood Concerns**

MAKING THE MOST OF THE GIRLS' BOOK

The activities and discussions in this session correspond with Chapter 2 of the girls' book, which focuses on the importance of being one's own best friend.

Pages 24–25, girls' book

MATERIALS

- **Opening Ceremony:** the symbols of friendship the girls bring
- **Putting a Value on Friendship:** chalkboard or whiteboard and writing implement
- **Framing the Sisterhood Smorgasbord with Friendship Values:** assorted art materials for decorating (see sidebar, page 39)
- **Sisterhood Snack:** any snacks the girls bring

Opening Ceremony: Symbols of Friendship

Gather the girls together and ask them to take turns presenting their individual items and explaining why they symbolize friendship.

36

Moving Into Your Social Style

Let the girls know that they'll now continue to explore their view of themselves—through a simple game that lets them consider their preferences in social situations.

Gather them together and ask that they stand one behind the other, single file in the middle of the room, all facing the same way. Explain that throughout this game, they will step to the right or left depending on how they feel about the instructions you call out. Let them know there's no right or wrong way to respond. What they do simply lets them learn more about themselves.

Then call out the scenes and the instructions below, one set at a time. If time allows, invite the girls to create their own scenarios, too, and take turns calling them out.

1 You're at a large party. Step to the left if you feel energized; step to the right if large parties drain your energy.

2 A woman approaches you in a coffee shop to ask about the yummy-looking dessert you're eating. Step to the left if you're comfortable talking to someone you don't know; step to the right if talking to someone new makes you uncomfortable.

3 You're visiting a new city by yourself. Step to the left if you're wishing you'd traveled with some friends; step to the right if you're having a great time.

4 You're working on a group project at school. Step to the left if you are taking the lead in moving the project forward; step to the right if you're happy to follow along with the decisions of your teammates.

5 You're on the soccer field and your teammate just scored. Step to the left if you're screaming and trying to lift her in the air; step to the right if you're running past and giving a quick high-five.

When the girls have run through all the scenes, have them take a look at where they're standing.

You might say: *These were extreme scenarios, but those who landed toward the left side of the room may tend to be more outgoing, and those who ended up on the right side of room may tend to be more reserved. There's no right way to be and rarely does anyone react in the same way to every situation.*

Then ask:

- *Why do you think we played this game? Why does it does it matter for our friendship and our sisterhood?*
- *When you think about your friends, are they more outgoing or more reserved? Or are they a combination of both?*

Then say something like:

- *Variety is the spice of life, and that's true in friendships, too! People's personality, character, and actions are more important than whether they show them in an outgoing way or a reserved way.*
- *In fact, the greatest leaders are comfortable with variety and diversity of any type. They're skilled at relating to all kinds of people!*

Putting a Value on Friendship

Now that the girls have an idea of their preferences and comfort levels in more general social situations, get them talking about what is most important to them in their friendships. You might say:

- *Now that you've seen how your social styles may vary, it's important to see how what we value in friendships may also vary.*
- *We might not find all our values in all of our friendships, but most likely we need certain values in our friendships to make those friendships true and authentic.*
- *For example, consider trust. You can't really have a friendship without it, can you?*

- *Likewise, we may have some values that are deal breakers for us: If we don't have these values in our friendships, those friendships can't move forward. In fact, they may just fizzle.*
- *An example of this may be maintaining a healthy lifestyle. For instance, if you find out that someone you thought was a friend abuses drugs or is violent toward others, you might question the value of that friendship.*
- *So let's take some time to think about what each of us values in our friendships.*

On a chalkboard or whiteboard, write the following question: *What do you value most in a friendship?* Then:

- Give each girl three index cards and a pen or pencil and invite her to write a word or phrase on her cards that best describes what she values most in a friendship.

- Ask a girl to collect the index cards and tape each value up on a board or wall. If some values were chosen by more than one girl, they can be taped down in one row to show how often they were valued in the group.

Now ask the girls to look over the friendship values. Start a discussion by acknowledging that there are likely some values listed that the girls hold but that didn't come to mind to all of them when they filled out their cards. Ask:

- Which values were most desired? Why do you think they ranked so high?
- Which values listed are not at all important to you? (Examples: sense of humor, intelligence, athletic interests)
- How many of the values listed echo the ones in the Girl Scout Law?
- Do you see how these values are worthwhile for all friendships, and for sisterhood in general?

Wrap up the discussion by saying something like: *When you're aware of what you value in friendships, you can better understand why a friendship may not be going the way you'd like. You may even be able to foresee when a friendship may fade.*

FRAMING THE SISTERHOOD SMORGASBORD WITH FRIENDSHIP VALUES

Suggest that the girls decorate their value cards with the art materials on hand and then use them to create a border or frame for the Sisterhood Smorgasbord they created in the last session.

Sisterhood Snack

Sharing Something of Ourselves
Now's the time for the Seniors to share the snacks they've brought.

Closing: Swapping Sisterhood Concerns

While the girls are enjoying their snacks, get them talking about issues of concern to each of them: issues that specifically affect women and girls—sisterhood issues. How to get them started? Ask them to walk through their day!

You might get them started by first asking some questions like these:

- What do you observe in your own daily life about how girls and/or women act as a sisterhood?
- What do you observe when girls/ women don't act like a sisterhood?
- What are some of the reasons at play when girls/women do or don't act like a sisterhood?
- When is something personal to you also a bigger issue that affects a larger sisterhood?

Next, get the Seniors recognizing sisterhood issues in their daily lives and in their community by asking them to think critically about all aspects of their day. You might say:

- *Start with when you wake up. What do you see or hear around you that could be improved for women and girls?*
- *What do you see/hear on the way to school?*
- *What do you see/hear at school?*
- *After school?*
- *In the evenings and on weekends?*

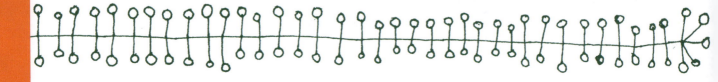

The girls might hit upon concerns raised in their book: girls being better friends to girls, girls being better able to defend themselves, girls needing better access to more opportunities at school and in life.

But if they are stuck for ideas or the conversation gets quiet, point them to some of the issues discussed in MISSION: SISTERHOOD! (see list on page 48 of this guide). Then get them brainstorming toward even more sisterhood concerns—ones that have meaning for them.

As they talk, they may come to realize that the issues they are concerned about are also issues of concern to other girls, maybe even all girls. As the girls name their various concerns, you might ask:

Do you think this issue is of concern to other girls, too—girls beyond our group of Seniors? Girls beyond our region?

Then say:

- *When we find an issue that reaches beyond our immediate group and that may be relevant for a larger group of girls, we may have found a sisterhood issue worth taking action on!*
- *Let's keep these issues in mind as we move forward in thinking about our steps to the Sisterhood Award.*

Looking Ahead to Session 3

Ask the girls to brainstorm a bit to decide on a television show (or movie, novel, play—any medium the girls like) they would like to view (or read) together at their next gathering. If one of the girls, or a member of your Network, has it on DVD, great. Otherwise check the Web for possible links via a network site or hulu.com.

Also ask the Network for assistance with ingredients and prep work for "Perfect Pairings."

STARTING IN ON THE SISTERHOOD AWARD

Sharing issues of concern is the Seniors first move toward the Sisterhood Award. The coaching tips on pages 42–43, and in later sessions, will help you guide the girls to a meaningful and rewarding project experience.

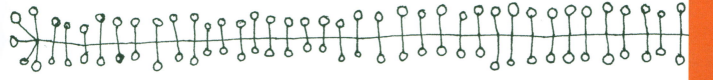

COACHING TIPS: WHAT MAKES A GREAT SISTERHOOD PROJECT?

Often, girls are involved in community projects that meet immediate needs (food, clothing, shelter) of others. Of course, these are all important. A Sisterhood Project is an opportunity to be involved in a new way: meeting the sometimes less obvious needs of girls and women, and creating a spiral of action that keeps on going. The impact of a Sisterhood Project has the potential to be large and long lasting. After all, if even one of the world's many sisterhood issues can be improved, then that alone can improve the lives of millions of girls and everyone those girls go on to inspire.

No matter what sisterhood issue the girls choose to earn the Sisterhood Award, keep in mind that it's not just what they do, but how they go about it and what they learn through trying that will inspire them to Take Action throughout their lives. Brainstorming and executing a Sisterhood Project gives girls planning skills that are valuable for any community project—and for so many other aspects of their lives.

As the girls zero in on their sisterhood issue and a plan for it, keep in mind these principles for a successful leadership award project:

The seniors' sisterhood issues . . .

A SUCCESSFUL PROJECT...

- **Meets a true sisterhood need** that the girls can observe and care about, and involves the girls in a specific solution—not so big and broad that they can't do it and feel the impact. Regardless of their interest, a little investigation will ensure that girls' efforts are spent on an area where they can make a difference for sisterhood—whether in their community or in the world.

- **Is realistic:** It's doable with the time and resources the girls have. Gently remind the girls to keep their effort focused around their time and resources. They will have more success that way and will see and feel their project's impact. To ensure that a project stays realistic, ask the girls about how it can fit in with their already busy lives. For example, can they incorporate it into their school day?

- **Allows girls to connect with others** and expand their sisterhood.

- **Uses the girls' talents and skills** in new ways. A great project allows all the girls to face a challenge—one they are excited and enthusiastic about.

- **Lets girls practice advocacy:** Speaking up is an important way to "do good." For example, the Seniors may need to present a plan to town officials to advocate for girls to have a baseball, not just a softball, team. Guide them to speak for themselves, even if adults don't take them seriously at first. You might step in to initiate a meeting, but then hand it back to the girls. Trying is what's most important: The girls will learn from their effort, no matter what the outcome.

- **Lets girls educate and inspire others** to be involved in their issue, too. This is an important way for girls to build confidence and realize that what they do really does matter. It also gives them a way to bring others into their project in order to make it sustainable (see next point!).

- **Strives for a sustainable impact:** That means the change girls start keeps on going!

- **Incorporates storytelling and creative expression,** the key themes of this journey. Encourage the girls to stretch themselves and make use of various creative methods they may not have tried before. Video? Photography? Dance? Online interactives? Go for it!

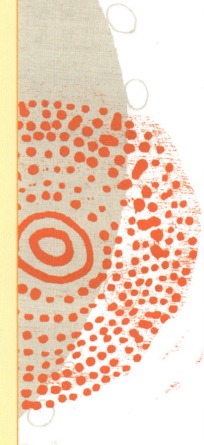

2 KNOW THYSELF

Figuring out friendships—of all kinds!—adds to the Seniors' growing confidence.

SAMPLE SESSION 3
With Friends Like These . . .

AT A GLANCE

Goal: The Seniors gain a better understanding of the importance various types and levels of friendships play in their lives.

- Opening Ceremony: What Kind of Friend Am I and When?
- Friendships on the Little Screen
- Further or Fizzle: Friendship Role-Play
- Sisterhood Snack: Perfect Pairings
- Creating a Short List for Sisterhood
- Closing Ceremony: Thank You, Sister!
- Project Planner

MAKING THE MOST OF THE GIRLS' BOOK

Chapter 1 of the girls' book, "Me + Friendship," will offer the girls a good background for the activities and discussions in this session.

Pages 10–11, girls' book

COACHING TOWARD THE SISTERHOOD AWARD

The girls get started on a short list of sisterhood issues in this session, so continue to make use of the Coaching Tips on page 42 to guide them to a meaningful project that will promote sustainable change. And use the Project Planner on pages 50–53 to keep track of all they accomplish.

MATERIALS

- **Friendships on the Little Screen:** DVD of TV show the girls plan to watch and DVD player and screen; or Web link and computer with Internet connection (if possible, projector and viewing screen)
- **Sisterhood Snack:** the food pairings your Network prepared
- **Creating a Short List for Sisterhood:** large piece of paper and marker, or chalkboard or whiteboard; copies of "What Makes a Great Sisterhood Project," page 49 of this guide

PREPARE AHEAD

- Set up the DVD or Web link for the TV show the girls have decided on for "Friendships on the Little Screen."
- Assemble or finish prepping ingredients for "Perfect Pairings."

44

Opening Ceremony: What Kind of Friend Am I and When?

Gather the girls in a circle and ask them to take turns answering the question, *What kind of friend am I?*, and give an example of when the friendship type they've identified comes through strongest. (Example: *I am a role model when my younger sister asks me for advice about a difficult situation.*)

Friendships on the Little Screen

Now's the time for the girls to watch the TV show (or watch/read another media of their choice) they've selected so they can identify and tally the types of friendships portrayed in it.

After the viewing, get the girls talking about what they've seen and tallied. You might ask:

- *Is it sometimes hard to label a friendship as just one type?*
- *Are some friendships several types? (For example, do confidante and mentor sometimes overlap in the same friendship?)*
- *When can friendships being more than one type pose difficulties? (Example: You're dating your lab partner and you break up right before the final experiment is due.)*
- *Which types of friendships do you see in your own life?*
- *Which types of friendship don't you have now but would like to add to your life?*

LET THE GIRLS DO THE NAMING

Pages 12–13 of the girls' book lists various types of friendships the Seniors are likely to encounter, and the different purposes often tied to friendships:

- acquaintance
- group friend
- good friend
- confidante
- networking friend
- role model
- mentor
- advisor

Keep these types and purposes handy as the girls hold their opening ceremony, but let the girls come up with their own friendship types—the list here is by no means definitive!

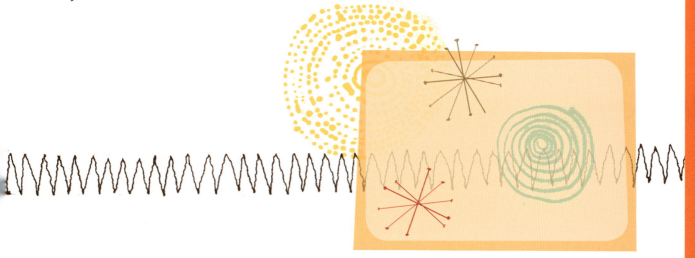

Further or Fizzle: Friendship Role-Play

Now turn the girls to focusing on levels of friendship, meaning the depth of closeness and trust within a particular friendship. Give them the suggested scenarios below (or they can create their own!) and ask them to take turns pairing up to role-play them.

1 You've just learned that **a friend in your ballet class has won a coveted spot in a recital** that you wanted. You've known her since grade school but you are starting to feel tired of being her runner-up.

2 **You return to the locker room after winning a big match** and find that a teammate you don't know so well has decorated your locker with all sorts of congratulatory notes and streamers.

3 **You really like a coworker at your weekend job at the mall.** She doesn't go to your school, but you have so much fun when you work together. You are always laughing but still get so much done.

4 **You just broke up with a significant other.** You really miss this person's support in your life, but you two have some issues that don't allow your romantic relationship to continue.

5 You hear a favorite teacher of yours, for whom you are an assistant, **using an ethnic slur in class**.

The scenarios are simple and quick, so encourage the girls to ham it up and really have fun with them.

While the pair plays out the scenario, the rest of the group will watch and decide whether this is a friendship that can go further or is destined to fizzle.

After a few minutes, freeze the scenario and ask the rest of the Seniors if this relationship is a "further" or a "fizzle"—and why. Ask:

- *Why is this relationship going in that direction? How is it going to play out and why? How can you take it further?*

- When a Senior starts to give a good rationale, say: *That sounds good! Come on up and take over for [one of the role-players] to finish this scenario in a way that naturally plays out what you've just explained.*

Remind the Seniors that there is no right or wrong ending to any of the scenarios, but they should always try to resolve the situation as directly as possible. You might say: *Being direct is a great leadership skill and one that's so useful in maintaining healthy relationships of all types. Remember, sometimes you further a friendship and it just gets a little deeper. But, sometimes, when you further a friendship you also further your sisterhood!*

Sisterhood Snack

Perfect Pairings

Did the girls enjoy the aMAZE leadership journey as Cadettes? If so, they may remember the "Snack Friends" named in their book. Invite them now to enjoy some famous "food friends" that you and the Network arranged as a snack for this gathering. You might introduce the snack pairings by saying: *Some good friends go together as well as the most famous food pairings. Think of peanut butter and jelly, rice and beans, bacon and eggs, cookies and milk, fish and chips, strawberries and cream.*

Creating a Short List for Sisterhood

Remind the girls of the sisterhood issues they raised at their last gathering. You might say:

We considered a number of issues that touch on all girls the last time we were together. After thinking about these sisterhood issues more, and any others you've heard or observed, which ones could most benefit from our taking action on them in our community?

Then hand out copies of "What Makes a Great Sisterhood Project?" and guide the girls to create a short list of sisterhood issues they feel passionate about—and could create some positive change on.

- As the list is created, ask the girls to assign themselves in small groups to each issue, so they can research and brainstorm further about whether their particular issue resonates in the community.

- Ask them to bring their findings, and any recommendations for taking action on issues that do resonate in their region, to the next gathering so they can consider them as a team.

IF THE GIRLS ARE STUCK FOR PROJECT IDEAS . . .

Refer them to the project examples throughout their book:

- **Finding the Beauty in Images of Beauty,** pages 20–23
- **Call Out That Inner Beauty!,** pages 32–35
- **Friendship Mentorship,** pages 43–45
- **Friendship Mixer,** pages 56–57

WHAT'S IMPORTANT? PLENTY OF TIME!

It's important to give the girls plenty of time to think about and share ideas as they explore Sisterhood Issues. They'll be more interested in their action project (and earning the Sisterhood Award) when they do something that really motivates them!

That's why you see time devoted to the girls' project selection over several sessions.

Then get them thinking critically about those examples. To do so, you might ask:

- *How does this example set a spiral in motion?*
- *How does it represent action that gets many people involved?*
- *How is it bigger than a one-time thing?*
- *What do you think about the underlying issue it addresses?*
- *In what other ways would you address this issue?*

Also get the girls thinking about the examples that most interest them by using the check sheet for "What Makes a Great Sisterhood Project?" (see opposite page). Can they see how a particular project example meets the criteria on the checklist? Can their own ideas fit these criteria, too?

If the girls don't have any issues of their own yet, encourage them to look around. What issues are on people's minds in their community? (Also see "Using the Time Capsule to Uncover Key Sisterhood Issues" at left to get the girls going on a Time Capsule event, as suggested in their book.)

At their next gathering, when the girls zero in on the issue they care most about, make use of the Project Planner on pages 50–53 to start tracking all that the girls decide and do.

Closing Ceremony: Thank You, Sister!

Gather the girls in a circle and ask them to take turns completing this sentence for the girl on their right: *I'm glad that you are part of my Senior sisterhood because . . .*

Looking Ahead to Session 4

Ask the girls to be sure to bring their cell phones to the next gathering. If some (or all) girls don't have cell phones, that's OK—"Modern Game of Telephone" can be played with just one phone or with paper!

Also talk with the girls about what "Packable Snacks" they might like for their next gathering (see page 58), and reach out to your Network for assistance with them.

USING THE TIME CAPSULE TO UNCOVER KEY SISTERHOOD ISSUES

Encourage the Seniors to have some fun with the Time Capsule event ideas on pages 60–61 of their book. They can reach out to girls in their region and beyond to learn about key sisterhood issues others may be concerned about. Issues that turn up as they prepare the group's time capsule might spur an idea for a great Sisterhood Project!

The girls might also hold a Time Capsule event as part of their final journey celebration. It will get them hearing about even more sisterhood issues and will spread the word about their own Sisterhood Project!

Pages 60–61, girls' book

Mission: Sisterhood!

WHAT MAKES A GREAT SISTERHOOD PROJECT?

Got some ideas for your Sisterhood Project? Run them through this Project Checklist and see if they meet all the criteria for a Sisterhood Project with impact! Simply ask, *Does my project idea . . .*

❑ **Meet a true need,** and involve me (and my team) in a specific solution that's not so big and broad that we can't do it and feel the impact?

❑ **Seem realistic** and is it doable with the time and resources I/we have? Can I fit this project into my busy life? How about my school day?

❑ **Allow me/my team to connect with others** and expand our sisterhood?

❑ **Use my/our talents and skills** in new ways? Does it allow me to face a challenge— one I'm excited and enthusiastic about?

❑ **Let me educate and inspire others** to be involved in this issue, too?

❑ **Strive for a sustainable impact?** Can the change I start keep on going?

❑ **Let me practice advocacy?** How?

❑ **Incorporate storytelling and creative expression?** Can I stretch myself to try a creative medium I have not tried before? Which one?

My Ideas . . .

Mission: Sisterhood!

PROJECT PLANNER

Our sisterhood issue:

Why we care about this issue:

Our goal (what we will do, and where and when):

How it will benefit sisterhood:

Mission: Sisterhood!

PROJECT PLANNER

Who we want to tap to join our project network/ expanded sisterhood	Area of expertise	Contact info

Mission: Sisterhood!

PROJECT PLANNER

Project tasks	Who does it?	When due?

Mission: Sisterhood!

PROJECT PLANNER

We'll educate and inspire _____ by . . .

We'll make use of these creative mediums . . .

Team-building skills we want to develop . . .

Being able to communicate well—that strengthens girls' confidence!

SAMPLE SESSION 4
Your Mission Starts Now!

AT A GLANCE

Goal: The Seniors get moving on their Sisterhood Project plan and explore how various forms of communication help or hinder friendships and sisterhood.

- Opening Ceremony: Sisterhood Forever!
- Zeroing in on a Sisterhood Issue
- Modern Game of Telephone
- Sisterhood Snacks: Packable Snacks
- Body-Language Charades
- Closing Ceremony: Shout Out for the Mission!

MATERIALS

- **Zeroing in on a Sisterhood Issue:** large sheet of paper or chalkboard or whiteboard and a writing implement
- **Modern Game of Telephone:** cell phone(s) with txting capability, or piece(s) of paper and pen(s)
- **Sisterhood Snacks:** (see page 58)
- **Body-Language Charades:** pen, slips of paper with moods (see Prepare Ahead, below), and bag or other container

PREPARE AHEAD

Write the suggested moods (in the sidebar on page 58), or others of your choice, on slips of paper for "Body-Language Charades."

MAKING THE MOST OF THE GIRLS' BOOK

Activities and discussions in this session correspond to Chapter 3 of the girls' book, "Buddy Up for Sisterhood." The girls may also find the Sisterhood Project Planner, on pages 68–77 of their book, useful at this stage of the journey.

Pages 36–37, girls' book

Opening Ceremony: Sisterhood Forever!

Gather the girls together and get them chanting: *Mission: Sisterhood! Yes! Mission: Impossible? Never! Why? Because sisterhood is forever!*

 ### Zeroing in on a Sisterhood Issue

Next, say something like:

Our sisterhood mission really gets moving today! We're going to try to zero in on a sisterhood issue we really care about and begin discussing the specifics of our Sisterhood Project. Our goal is to select an issue where we can create some lasting change!

Get the girls going with a chart of the ideas from the short list they created at their last gathering. Have each "idea team" present its research and recommendations and then encourage the girls to weigh all the project ideas that the various teams raise.

 As the discussion moves forward, guide the girls to weigh the feasibility of their various project ideas by asking questions like these:

- *How could this issue allow us to create change?*
- *Who could most benefit from this change?*
- *Who else might our change affect in a positive way?*
- *What resources (people, materials, equipment) might this change require?*
- *What time is needed to accomplish this change with the resources we have available?*

1 TEAM, 2 TEAMS, 3 TEAMS, 4?

As high school students, the Seniors are mature enough and passionate enough to take on their own sisterhood issues. So they might want to team up on different Sisterhood Projects. Two girls might take on one issue, while three other girls take on a separate issue. What's important is that the girls tackle issues they are passionate about.

If the girls aren't ready to pick an issue, they may want to talk to more people in their community. Who might they invite as a guest speaker? Who might they visit on a field trip?

4 YOUR MISSION STARTS NOW!

55

> **"FIST TO FIVE"**
>
> In this way of reaching consensus, everyone starts by holding up a tightly closed fist, and as opinions are expressed about what the group might do, each girl uses her fingers to do the talking. Depending on how many fingers are showing, the group either continues discussing the issue or moves ahead in agreement.

After weighing the possible results and the feasibility of each project idea, the Seniors will be ready to select the project they will do. If opinions vary, suggest that they aim for a consensus.

- If the girls were once Juniors and took the *Agent of Change* leadership journey, you might say: *Remember "Fist to Five"? It still works!*

- *Keep in mind that when you reach a consensus, it means that everyone in the group can support the same decision or agree to live with it. Building consensus is a great skill to have—it's something all great leaders strive to do.*

Once the Seniors have decided on a project, point them to the Sisterhood Project Planner in their book, where they can begin stepping out a project plan.

Let them know they'll spend time planning together when they next gather. Then congratulate them by saying something like:

- *We've really taken off on our mission today. You made good use of your leadership skills! You'll continue to use them on your mission, in all your friendships, and throughout life.*

- *Already today you may have tried out your consensus-building skills. Now let's test some other communication skills that can help on this mission, and in all you do.*

- *We've touched on the importance of speaking honestly and directly in our relationships. That's not always easy!*

Then say something like:

We communicate in other ways, too. One of them is something you probably do all the time—txting!

And then move directly into "Modern Game of Telephone."

Modern Game of Telephone

Ask the girls how much they txt. Is the answer "a lot"?

Ask them to sit in a circle with their phones and each write a brief txt message, not more than 140 characters, describing an incident. Give the girls 45 seconds to write their txt. If they need an example, you might offer: *Drew @ mall w/Mina she lks mad. its over. he cheats & failed calc.*

- Ask the girls to copy their message on a piece of paper for recall at end of the game.

- Next, ask each girl to pass her phone to the girl to her right, who will look at the txt for not more than 10 seconds, erase it, and recompose it in her own words before handing the phone to the next girl. And on it goes, until all girls have participated on all phones and the phones are back with their original owners.

- Then have the girls take turns reading aloud the final txt they "received" and the original txts they wrote at the start of the game. Go around the room until all final and original messages have been compared in this way.

Next, get a discussion going among the girls about whether or not the original txt and the final one match up. Start with questions like these:

- *What patterns are you seeing with the txts? How were you passing on accurate or inaccurate information or misreading the txts you received?*

- *Which messages were completely off base?*

- *If you have had a "mis-message" happen to you in real life, how did you handle it?*

- *What effect did the "mis-message" have? Did it alter one of your friendships in any way?*

- *When have you written a txt you wish you hadn't? How did you deal with it?*

- *If you received a false or hurtful txt, how would you deal with it? Would you confront the sender? Would you ignore it and simply hit delete?*

NO PHONES NEEDED

This game can be played directly on the girls' cell phones without incurring any costs because the Seniors can compose and erase without ever pressing "send." The girls can use one phone and pass it around or they can use multiple phones—or if all the girls brought phones, they can each start with a phone. The more phones, the more fun!

If cell phones are not available, the girls can write their txts on paper. (The paper can be passed around, with each girl reading the txt for not more than five seconds, folding the paper over, and then rewriting the message.)

TO TXT OR NOT

Ask the girls to come up with a list of sensitive situations or messages that are best not to txt, such as:

- criticizing someone
- breaking up with a significant other
- a joke that might not "read" as a joke and instead might make the recipient feel attacked and disrespected

THINK B4 U SEND

Encourage the girls to create a mental checklist to run through before hitting "send," and perhaps a slogan ("Think B4 U Send") or acronym that helps them remember the checklist, like 3R's:

Review: Is my txt clear?

Recipient: Am I sending this to the right person?

Ready: Am I sure I want to send this?

YOUR MISSION STARTS NOW!

57

sisterhood snack

Packable Snacks

Invite the girls to rest and refuel with easy-to-eat fruit, low-fat mozzarella cheese sticks, crackers—anything that doesn't require utensils or elaborate preparation and can be packed and taken on a mission! Let the girls choose!

Body-Language Charades

Let the girls know that communication, in all its many forms, is important. You might say:

- *You've just spent some time txting. We also communicate all the time in another way: with our bodies.*
- *The way we stand, how we hold our arms, whether we roll our eyes— these all send out messages to those around us.*
- *So let's play a little game to see how accurately we can send out and decode messages via body language alone.*
- *Ever played charades where you guessed the name of a celebrity or a show? Well, we're going to play charades about moods!*

Then pull out the bowl or bag of moods (that you created from the suggested moods at left) and say:

- *So, no words allowed! Just pick a slip of paper and we'll take turns acting out a mood while the rest of us try to guess it.*

LARGE GROUP? TRY TEAM CHARADES

Depending on the size of your group, the Seniors might choose to play mood charades in teams. Each player on a team selects one mood to act out. One at a time, the girls take turns acting out the mood they picked. When the mood is guessed correctly, the next player on the team steps up to act out a mood. The first team to guess all its moods wins!

SUGGESTED MOODS AND FEELINGS

- Excited
- Elated
- Angry
- Nervous
- Bored
- Frustrated
- Tired
- Happy
- Confident
- Sleepy

To wrap up the game, you might ask:

- *How did we do? Were we good communicators? Why or why not?*
- *Who can remember a time when you misinterpreted a friend's body language? What happened?*

 ### Closing Ceremony: Shout Out for the Mission!

Invite the girls to think up their own version of the Sisterhood chant that opened this session. Two or three easy-to-remember lines are all they need. Then have the Seniors pump up the volume and chant for sisterhood!

Looking Ahead to Session 5

Ask the girls to dress to move for their next gathering. That means athletic clothing, or anything loose and comfortable, and sneakers. Let the girls choose which active activity they prefer.

Reach out to your Network for ingredients for One Sweet Salsa (see page 62).

Strength and fitness—both get girls feeling capable and confident!

SAMPLE SESSION 5
Fit for the Mission

AT A GLANCE

Goal: The Seniors learn ways to keep their relationships, minds, and bodies healthy and fit as they move forward with their Sisterhood Project.

- **Opening Ceremony: Laughter Parade**
- **Friends and Our Health**
- **Sisterhood Snack: One Sweet Salsa**
- **Planning the Sisterhood Project**
- **Friendships Keep Us Fit**
- **Closing Ceremony: Thanking Our Bodies**

MAKING THE MOST OF THE GIRLS' BOOK

Activities and discussions in this session correspond to Chapters 1 and 2 of the girls' book, "Me + Friendship" and "Be My Own Best Friend"—especially "A Long-Running and Healhty Friendship" and "Body Buddies," on pages 18–19 and 27. The Sisterhood Project Planner, on pages 68–77 of their book, will also come in handy.

Pages 18–19, girls' book

MATERIALS

- **Friendships and Our Health:** chalkboard or whiteboard, or larger sheet of paper, and a writing implement
- **Sisterhood Snack: One Sweet Salsa** (see page 62)
- **Friendships Keep Us Fit:** a sticky note and pen or pencil for each girl
- **Closing Ceremony:** sticky notes, at least three or four for each girl; pens or pencils

PREPARE AHEAD

Secure a location for "Friendships Keep Us Fit" (see page 63).

 Opening Ceremony: Laughter Parade

Ask the girls to stand in a circle and begin to walk slowly in the same direction, throwing up their arms and laughing as they go.

60

- Let them know they may have to fake their laughter at first.
- After one complete circle, ask them to speed up their walking—and their laughter—and walk the circle two more times. Pretty soon, their fake laughter will become real giggles and laughs.

Afterward, start a discussion with questions like these:

- *How would you describe your mood before you started walking and laughing?*
- *How would you describe your mood and attitude during the laughter exercises? After?*
- *If your mood changed, do you think laughing out loud was responsible for the change?*
- *When was the last time you had a "hold-your-stomach, I-can't-breathe" laughter fit. What was it about? Was it with friends? Family members?*
- *Where does sense of humor rank on your list of friendship values?*

Wrap up by letting the girls know that humor and laughter are often a welcome aspect of friendships, and a way for girls to bond with one another.

Friends and Our Health

Next, ask the girls: *How do our friends keep us healthy?*

Then say: *Let's brainstorm a list:* (Possible answers: They encourage us to eat well, exercise, and avoid "toxic" substances, practices, and people; they support us in good times and in bad.)

Once the girls have a full list going, ask them to consider whether their friends do these things for their friends, whether their friends do these things for them, and whether they do these things for themselves. You might say:

How good are we at following our own advice? Can we come up with some ways to better follow our own list of healthy encouragements? After all, when it comes to health, we should always be our own best friend!

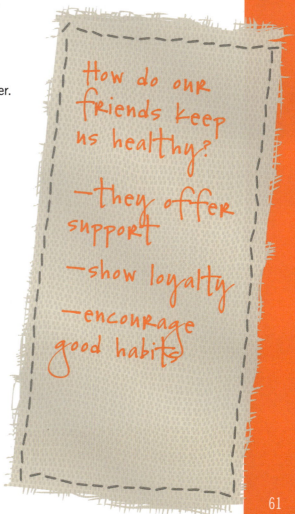

Sisterhood Snack

ONE SWEET SALSA

Bring out the snack ingredients and let the Seniors team up for some healthy bonding and eating by chopping, mixing, and then digging into their Sisterhood Salsa.

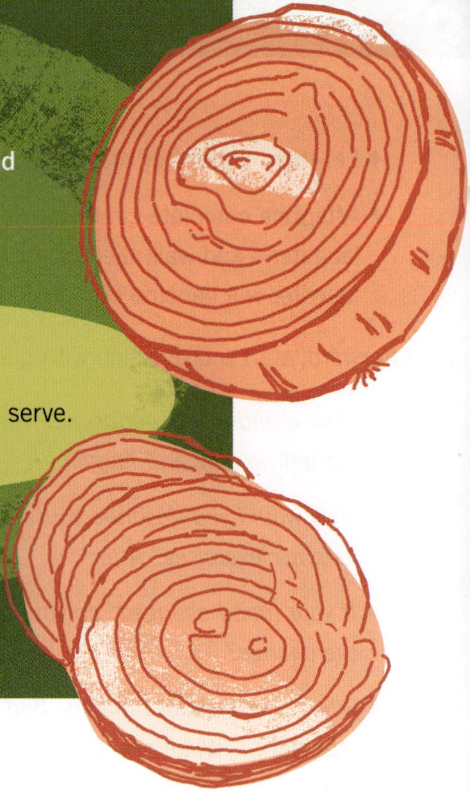

WHAT YOU NEED:

- 2 cups chopped watermelon
- 1/2 cup chopped mango
- 4 ounces goat cheese
- 2 tablespoons chopped red onion
- Generous handful fresh torn cilantro
- 2 tablespoons fresh lime juice
- Black pepper to taste
- Corn tortilla chips for dipping

INSTRUCTIONS:

Combine all ingredients and serve.

Planning the Sisterhood Project

Remind the girls that at their last gathering they decided on a sisterhood issue to Take Action on. Let them know that now is the time to think about a realistic scale and scope for the project. Encourage them to consider which creative medium(s) will allow them to best educate and inspire others on their issue, or which will let them advocate for the change they want to see. Point them to the Project Planner in their book, where they can also step through any budget concerns, publicity ideas, and ways to expand their network by engaging others as volunteers or mentors. Be sure to share with them the Networking tips on page 75 of this guide, and use the Sisterhood Planner (pages 50–53) to keep track of all the girls are doing.

Friendships Keep Us Fit

Introduce this activity by saying, *Laughter is said to be the best medicine, and what we did at the start of our time together seems to prove that. No matter how we felt going into it, we mostly felt pretty good after our laughter parade, right?*

- *Our mission on this journey is an important one, and we need to stay healthy and fit to achieve it! How do we do that?*
- *Through our own friendships! The best friendships and relationships keep us healthy. And I'm not just talking about physical health here, but social and emotional health, too.*
- *I'm sure you can all guess that these three aspects of our well-being are interrelated!*
- *Now, let's get outdoors and see just how connected they are.*

Once outside, have the girls spend about 15 minutes doing an active activity of their choice (see sidebar at right).

After the activity, gather the girls together and give each one a sticky note and pen or pencil, and ask her to write one word that describes how she feels right now (sample words the girls might write: exhilarated, exhausted, out of shape, fit, tired, slow, strong, lazy, beautiful, healthy, unhealthy, flabby, bored).

Then have all the girls fold their sticky notes over and hand them to you.

Read the words on the sticky notes aloud, and get the girls to place them in two piles, according to whether the words are mostly positive, or mostly negative. Then depending on how the piles stack up, say something like:

- *First, let's consider the negative words that came out of this. Someone wrote _____, someone else wrote _____, and a third girl wrote _____ .*
- *Why do we think some of us had these reactions? Were we worried about how we looked? What we're wearing? Or did we just have something else on our minds that kept us from enjoying the moment?*
- *How about the positive words here? Do these reflect that some us felt fit and strong? Energized? Were we paying any attention to our strength? Our speed? Our stamina? Were we focused and in the moment?*

ACTIVE ACTIVITY? THE GIRLS CHOOSE!

Ask the Seniors to choose one of these activities (or another equally active option of their choice)

- Run an indoor or outdoor track
- Go for a swim
- Take a hike
- Do a fast walk five times around the block
- Play a yoga tape and do yoga together
- Do a dance workout

DIFFERENTLY ABLED GIRLS EMBRACE ACTIVITY, TOO!

Keep in mind that physical activities can focus on individual body parts as well as the whole body. For example, a dance might involve only arms and hands or a hike can be taken in wheelchairs on paved paths. Search the Web for fun ideas!

Then sum up this part of the discussion by making points like these:

- We all have different feelings when we engage in physical activity. Some of us like it and thrive on it; others would rather avoid it.

- How we feel when we engage in physical activity might really say more about how we feel about our bodies than how healthy or athletic we actually are.

- When we focus on our bodies as strong, functional, and fit, we are more likely to enjoy engaging in physical activity. We see our bodies in a positive way.

- But when we focus on whether our body is attractive or not, we aren't appreciating its many capabilities. That can limit our physical performance. More important, it can limit our emotional health. It has the power to make us feel bad. We may even avoid physical activity, and end up not making healthy choices in other areas of our lives.

Closing Ceremony: Thanking Our Bodies

Now, depending on what physical activity the girls just did, say something like:

- For our closing today, let's take a moment to appreciate something about our bodies.

- Did your lungs keep you going around that track? Did your legs keep you moving? Did you show amazing balance or flexibility? Did you have great rhythm? Choose anything you'd like to appreciate, even your little toe!

- Take another sticky note and write a one-line thank-you to your body or a part of your body that kept up with this physical activity.

- Hold on to your thank-you note, take it home, and post it where you will see it the most—maybe on a bathroom mirror or a bedside lamp. Let it serve as a reminder of all your body is capable of doing for you every day.

Wrap up by saying: *Focusing on your body as strong, fit, and capable is important for this journey and its sisterhood mission—and it's also important for your life!*

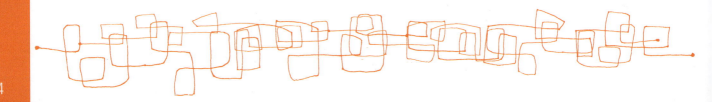

Looking Ahead to Sessions 6 & 7

Call on your Network to assemble a random group of objects—things the Seniors will recognize but not necessarily all consider beautiful. For example, consider a household plant, a teakettle, a lamp shade, a mirror, a purse, an umbrella, a bracelet, a beach ball, a feather, an MP3 player, a water bottle, a vase, a piece of fruit or a vegetable, a poster, a magazine cover, a locket, a pair of sunglasses. Be sure to have more objects than girls in your group.

Ask the girls to each bring in some loose buttons—one for each sister Senior. Buttons can be found in the family sewing basket, on clothing no longer being worn, or on the inside panel of a new shirt. Also, check the Materials list for Buddy Button Bracelets (page 66), and reach out to your Network for any other supplies the girls will need.

If the girls will be making a Diversity Salad (see page 69), ask them to each bring one ingredient, chopped or otherwise ready to eat, that will be combined into a team salad. Encourage the girls to include greens, herbs, vegetables, fresh or dried fruits, and nuts and cheese (check for allergies first!). Plan for a simple lemon-juice-and-olive-oil dressing (1 part lemon juice, 2 parts olive oil, pepper and/or salt to taste).

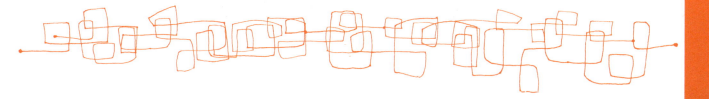

SAMPLE SESSIONS 6 & 7
Sisterhood Knows No Boundaries

LET THE SENIORS DECIDE & DIVIDE THEIR PROJECT TIME

Sessions 6 & 7 are set aside as time for the Seniors to focus on their Sisterhood Project. Depending on the time the girls have and the nature of their sisterhood issue, they might be doing their project for one or two, or more sessions. Use the tips on page 75 to guide the girls in planning projects that will go beyond helpful, one-time events to address root causes of an issue and achieve sustainable change.

The activities offered here can be enjoyed apart from, and along with, their project.

MAKING THE MOST OF THE GIRLS' BOOK

The activities and discussions in these two project-centered Sample Sessions correspond to Chapter 4 of the girls' book, "Friendship Without Borders." And, of course, the Sisterhood Project Planner will come in handy as well.

Pages 46–47, girls' book

AT A GLANCE

Goal: The Seniors team up and carry out their efforts to have a positive impact on the sisterhood issue they chose en route to earning the Sisterhood Award.

- Opening Ceremonies: How Long Is a Conga Line?/ Huddle for Sisterhood
- Beauty Is in the Eye of the Beholder
- Meditation: How Our Network Changed Me
- Sisterhood Snacks: Peas in a Pod, Diversity Salad
- Careers in Advocacy
- Buddy Button Bracelets
- Closing Ceremonies: Finish This Sisterhood Sentence!

MATERIALS

- **Opening Ceremonies: How Long Is a Conga Line:** music of the girls' choosing and a music player
- **Beauty Is in the Eye of the Beholder:** objects collected by you and your Network
- **Sisterhood Snacks:** see page 69
- **Careers in Advocacy:** computer and Internet connection (or meet at a library)
- **Buddy Button Bracelets:** buttons the girls bring in; cloth, leather, elastic, string, ribbon, or cord; thread, glue; and any other material of the girls' choosing

PREPARE AHEAD

Organize the objects you and your Network collected for "Beauty Is in the Eye of the Beholder," and assemble supplies for the "Buddy Button Bracelets."

If the girls plan to have a Diversity Salad (see page 69), prepare the dressing, set out utensils, and gather anything else needed, including a bowl large enough to hold all of the girls' ingredients.

Opening Ceremonies: How Long Is a Conga Line?

Gather the girls together, turn on the music the girls chose to bring, and ask them to start a conga line! Have one person start it on her own. Not so fun, right? Have second girl join in. Still not great, right? It's not even a line yet! So get all the girls dancing—now, that's a conga line!

HUDDLE FOR SISTERHOOD

Ask the girls to huddle and pile up their right hands one on top of the other. Then give them 30 seconds to come up with one word, which they'll shout out when they lift up their hands, that signifies their hopes for team unity on this project (the word can't be *sisterhood*!).

Beauty Is in the Eye of the Beholder

Gather the girls together and start this activity with points like these:

- *By expanding our network, we hopefully also expand our ways of thinking and our view of the world.*

- *We may hold very strong views on many aspects of life, but that doesn't mean we can't respect, and consider, differing viewpoints—which others may hold just as strongly as we hold our own.*

- *Take beauty, for example. We all have our own notions of what is beautiful. Think of the variety of beauty in the world—in art and in nature. Certainly some objects and landscapes are beautiful to some people but not to others.*

- *It's always nice when our own notions of beauty are shared by others, but does it really matter whether anyone else agrees with our ideals of beauty? Can't we enjoy what we consider beautiful no matter whether anyone else does or not? Isn't beauty in the eye of the beholder?*

- *Of course, that doesn't mean we shouldn't let ourselves be open to considering new ideals of beauty, and new ways of thinking about and seeing the world.*

67

Now, ask the girls to sit in a circle and place all the objects your Network collected in the center.

- Give each girl a slip of paper and ask them to all write down which object they think is most beautiful, and why (its shape, color, size, use, a memory it triggers, etc.).
- Then ask the girls to fold the slip of paper but keep it in front of them.
- Next, ask the girls to go around the circle showing their answers to group, and explaining why the object is beautiful to them.

Then say something like:

- *Sometimes we share common notions of beauty but more often we don't—or we may find the same thing beautiful but for different reasons. For example, I might like this lamp shade best because of what it does, but some of you might like it for its color and fabric.*
- *The reverse of this is true, too. We might all agree that the color blue is beautiful, but some of us might prefer a deep blue, like the one in this poster, and others might prefer a lighter, transparent blue, like the blue of this glass vase, or the blue of the sea.*
- *This is true of other things we consider beautiful, too. Beauty goes so much beyond the physical and the observable. Think of relationships, stories, music—anything in life you might call beautiful.*

You might ask:

- *How do these various notions of beauty play out in your own life?*
- *Do you stay true to your own notions of beauty when you decide what to wear to school? When you read a fashion magazine?*
  - *Have your notions of beauty ever clashed with those of your friends? What was the result? How did you react? Did you conform to match your friends or did you stick with your own ideals?*

Meditation: How Our Network Changed Me

At any point along the project, it might be helpful to ask the Seniors to take some time to think quietly, on their own, about how the diversity of backgrounds and experiences among their expanded team has helped them create the best possible project and also expanded their view of themselves and the world. Ask them to meditate on these questions:

- *What has been most challenging for you about expanding this network?*

- *Did any of your opinions shift when you started hearing ideas from new members of our expanded project team?*

- *Were your eyes opened to new ways of doing things when people you've never worked with before began to offer their ideas to the project mix?*

- *What new things have you learned with this group so far that you want to take with you to use in other areas of life?*

- *How can your expanded network help you in your life?*

chat time!

Sisterhood Snack

PEAS IN A POD

The girls might be interested to know that when it comes to peas, the more peas in a pod, the sweeter the peas! For this fresh and easy Sisterhood Snack, serve up a bunch of fresh or frozen (organic if you can!) peas in the pod: garden peas or sweet peas, sugar snaps, snow peas—whatever you can find. They can be eaten raw or steamed quickly in a microwave. If desired, serve them with hummus or another healthful dip.

DIVERSITY SALAD

Just as a diversity of people enrich our lives (and our Sisterhood Project!), a diversity of ingredients makes for an interesting and more delicious salad. Just have the girls combine their ingredients in a large bowl and serve with a simple lemon-juice-and-olive-oil dressing (see page 65).

LIKE TO KEEP IT FRESH AND LOCAL?

Then encourage the girls to dip into *SOW WHAT?*, from the *It's Your Planet: Love It!* series of leadership journeys. This journey gives Seniors the opportunity to explore their "food print" and their "leader print," all with the aim of benefitting their own and the planet's health.

6&7

SISTERHOOD KNOWS NO BOUNDARIES

BE AN ADVOCATE NOW, FOR GIRLS!

The GSUSA Public Policy and Advocacy Office, based in Washington, D.C., advocates for issues affecting the Girl Scout Movement and girls. Its staff members serve as a voice for girls with the White House, Capitol Hill, and other policy makers, which means they're making sure your perspective is heard by and influencing lawmakers!

But you don't have to wait to start your career to advocate! To participate in Girl Scouts' many advocacy efforts, join the Girl Scout Advocacy Network at girlscouts4girls.org.

SENIORS READY FOR MORE ADVOCACY?

If the girls are passionate about an issue and want to make sure their message gets heard, let them know they have plenty to look forward to as Ambassadors taking the *Your Voice, Your World: The Power of Advocacy* journey. This leadership journey invites Ambassadors to speak up and speak out for positive change.

Careers in Advocacy

Get this activity started by saying something like:

- *You've educated and inspired others on your sisterhood issue, but another way to Take Action for sisterhood is to advocate for a sisterhood issue. In this way, you are taking action for sisters you haven't even met!*

- *In fact, many women make careers out of advocating for issues for women and girls around the world.*

Some of the women and girls featured throughout the girls' book have tackled issues the girls might not ordinarily think about. And by now, the Seniors have also met some new adults through their own networking who may be focused on other issues of personal concern.

Say something like: *Sometimes you can really widen your reach through advocacy. Perhaps there was an issue you considered for your Sisterhood Project but you had to scale back to something closer to home. If you could have a career where you could reach wider, what career would you choose?*

Grants manager? Researcher? Social worker? Working for a nonprofit that supports girls and women? (That's a nearly unlimited choice of positions from marketing to fund-raising!)

Get the girls to huddle around a computer, either at your meeting space or at a library, to search out what kinds of advocacy jobs are available at organizations they might be interested in.

- ❏ The girls might research organizations that advocate for girls and women and search career, internship, and fellowship opportunities there. For example, they could go to the CARE Web site and click on the Careers link. What current jobs openings are posted? Which ones might interest them? Which make use of skills they have or would like to develop?

- ❏ Or the girls might find an organization advocating for an issue they care about. Encourage them to connect with the organization to form a Girl Advisory Council that could add the "girl perspective" to its activities and advocacy initiatives.

GIRLS' APPETITES WHETTED? GIVE THEM MORE!

Encourage the Seniors to research women in your state or community who do advocacy work. You might offer them some questions like these, so they can come back and share what they've learned with the full group:

- *Who are these women and where do they work?*
- *What issues do they advocate on?*
- *How do they advocate?*

The girls might also ask to shadow an advocate for a day to learn about her job and how she started doing advocacy work.

If they haven't already, the Seniors might want to let some of these advocates know about the sisterhood issues they're taking action on for this journey. The girls might consider gaining their support by e-mailing, calling, or meeting with them.

6&7 SISTERHOOD KNOWS NO BOUNDARIES

WHAT STYLE BRACELET?

Let the girls decide! They might sew their buttons on a cloth, leather, or elastic cuff, tie them together with macramé knots, simply string them on a thin cord or ribbon, or use any creative method they can think of based on the materials you, the girls, and your Network have gathered. Some girls might even create a pattern with their buttons—perhaps a flower or spiral!

If any girls want to go all out, they might continue their handiwork between sessions and then share their creations at their next gathering.

GET CREATIVE

Buddy Button Bracelets

Ask the girls to bring out the buttons they're brought with them. Share with them the idea that buttons can be more than just fasteners for fabric. They can also serve as symbols of the connection we have to close friends or our sisters. Say something like:

- *In Victorian times, young girls collected buttons to make what were called "charm strings" or "memory strings" that they used to remind them of special occasions or visits from friends and family members.*

- *Now we're going to carry on something of that tradition by making Buddy Button Bracelets that can always remind us of the sisterhood we shared on this journeys.*

- *So, the buttons we give one another won't simply fasten our clothes together. With these bracelets, they will "fasten" us to our sisterhood circle! What a nice notion!*

Invite the girls to give one button to each of their sister Seniors. Then, they can begin fashioning a bracelet in the style of their choice, whether thin or cuff style (see ideas at left).

Conclude by saying something like:

- *Sometimes simple things have lots of meaning and lots of sentimental value.*
- *Let these bracelets serve as mementos of our time together on this journey and our ongoing connection to our Girl Scout sisterhood.*

Be sure to encourage the girls to wear their Buddy Button Bracelets at the journey's final celebration!

Closing Ceremonies: Finish this Sisterhood Sentence!

Each time the girls gather to work on their Sisterhood Project, you might suggest that they close their time together by gathering in a circle and taking turns completing one of these sentences:

- *Our project is meaningful because . . .*

- *This project inspires me to . . .*

- *Our project helps our sisterhood by . . .*

Looking Ahead to Session 8

Ask the girls to search out a "Sisterhood Story" to share at their next gathering—not a full story but a selected paragraph, or line(s) that carry special significance for them. These stories can be taken from any media: novels, poetry, movies, TV, advertising, etc.

Reach out to your Network for materials for "Thanking Our Sisterhood Circle" and the Sisterhood "Tea" (see page 78 for both).

COACHING TIPS: NETWORKING FOR SISTERHOOD

Through their Sisterhood Project, girls are seeing themselves as leaders who address their own needs and the needs of others and rally people together in the process. These coaching tips will help you guide the Seniors to make the most *of sisterhood* as they advocate *for sisterhood*:

☐ **Whom can you meet?** New people = new ideas + new opportunities. That's what sisterhood is all about. As the girls' project takes shape, guide them to search out who can assist them best with their efforts. What might they learn from talking to local artists, educators, or social workers? The more people the girls meet, the more authentic and purposeful their projects will be! Ask the girls and their families who they know, and who those people know. You don't need to know everyone on your own!

☐ **Consider the power of more girls:** What are other Girl Scouts, especially Seniors, doing in your region to improve sisterhood? Perhaps others on the *MISSION: SISTERHOOD!* journey can offer new ideas, new perspectives, and new opportunities—for the project and for life!

☐ **Greater numbers, greater sustainability?** The more interest, experience, and people power behind a project, the greater the chance that the change the project aims for will be lasting. So guide the girls to expand their network with an eye for who can really support their issue and keep the change going. Sharing their project, in big or small ways, gives them a chance to give others a call to action and that's a great way to make your project's impact sustainable! Would younger girls benefit from knowing about the project? Families? Consider a presentation at school or at a place of worship, or online networking.

☐ **Group dynamics of an expanding network:** Take every chance that comes up to give the girls constructive feedback about their efforts as a team and to coach them through any difficulties (with communication, decision-making, scheduling conflicts, opinions) that arise. You might also talk with them about how the size of their team, which may grow as their network grows, may affect its working dynamic. Do more teammates call for new ways of teaming up? Do more teammates call for greater clarity of individual roles?

☐ **Take time to talk about it!** Taking time to talk about what they're doing, on their own, as a team, and for sisterhood, is an important part of the girls' learning experience. What is hard? Why? What does it take to work around a challenge? What will they miss if they give up? If a plan is not working, how can they adjust it? What is fun about this project? What are the Seniors most proud of?

When Seniors see how sisterhood shapes their stories, they feel supported and confident.

SAMPLE SESSION 8
Making Sisterhood Your Story!

LOOKING OUT, LOOKING IN
Now that the Seniors have completed their Sisterhood Project, they turn their focus inward—on their own sisterhood story.

AT A GLANCE

Goal: The Seniors apply all they have explored to their own understanding of how sisterhood has shaped, and will continue to shape, their life stories.

- Opening Ceremony: Sisterhood Stories
- Sisterhood Stories Take Center Stage
- Thanking Our Sisterhood Circle
- Sisterhood Snack: Tea and Sandwiches
- Closing Ceremony: Seasoning the Smorgasbord

MATERIALS

- **Opening Ceremony:** Whatever each girl has chosen to share
- **Sisterhood Stories Take Center Stage:** paper and pencils or pens.
- **Thanking Our Sisterhood Circle:** paper or other material of the girls' choice, plain paper, pens and pencils, gingerbread women (or men!), cookie cutters, glue, scissors.
- **Sisterhood Snack:** (see page 78)

PREPARE AHEAD
Get the Seniors involved in setting up materials for "Thanking Our Sisterhood Circle" and ingredients for the Sisterhood "Tea."

Opening Ceremony: Sisterhood Stories

Gather the girls together and ask them to take turns sharing their "Sisterhood Story" excerpts, whether a short paragraph from a book, a line from a poem, a bit of dialogue from a movie, a slogan from an ad—or whatever they've chosen to share.

GET CREATIVE

Sisterhood Stories Take Center Stage

In this activity, the Seniors brainstorm together and then each girl writes a one-act play that sums up how sisterhood has shaped her life story up to this point. This lets each girl see what she's gained along the journey and how sisterhood might continue to inform her future and her potential in life.

Remind the girls their play will be based on real life, but that they'll be altering one aspect (the characters, the time, the setting) to give their plays a fictional twist.

Explain the activity to the girls and then say something like:

- *We'll start this as a group, so you can brainstorm ideas together and then you'll split up and write your plays on your own.*

- *You might even go outside to lounge under a tree as you write. Or we could play some music while you write indoors.*

Then get the girls started with these playwriting tips:

- ❑ A play relies on characters, situation, and theme all working together. These plays are about you, your life, and your sisterhood. All three need to combine smoothly in your play.

- ❑ Keep it simple: This is a short play (one act) that you need to write quickly, so limit the number of characters, and use just one setting.

- ❑ Settle on your plot first; that's what's most important. Make sure yours comes to a resolution! Then focus in on specifics, like dialogue.

- ❑ And write with passion! If you aren't moved by your own story, no one else will be!

- ❑ When the girls are done you might encourage their creativity by saying: Did you enjoy this? Then write the next act—and the act after that!

ALTER THE STORY, MAKE IT YOUR OWN!

Asking the girls to fictionalize at least one aspect of their story (characters, time line, or setting), lets them:

- add in some creativity
- control the course of events
- use an element of anonymity, which may make the stories easier to share.

ACT 'EM OUT!

If the girls are excited to share their stories and they have the time, encourage them to go all out and perform their one-act plays (or record them to share later in any media they choose).

They could share a live performance, or a recording, with other sisters—younger, older, or peers—at a special gathering. Or they might do it at their final celebration, so all their guests can enjoy the stories, too.

MAKING SISTERHOOD YOUR STORY

GET CREATIVE

Thanking Our Sisterhood Circle

Ask the girls to think about all the people they've talked to and learned from along this journey—from women they might have invited to a session as guest speakers to everyone who helped to move their Sisterhood Project forward (even the adults who drove them to their Senior gatherings!).

How might they thank them for their sisterhood? How can they express how much their interest and time has meant?

Here's a way: Send them Sisterhood thank-you notes shaped like a sisterhood!

The notes will look extra special if the girls create them from vintage wallpaper, newsprint, wrapping paper, even felt or fabric. Any materials that can't be easily written on can be backed with plain paper.

1 To get started, have each girl choose a sheet of paper from the available materials. Make a square a little bit larger than the size you want for your final circle.

2 Place the paper patterned-side down. Fold along the diagonal to make a triangle. Fold the triangle in half and in half again to make a smaller triangle.

sisterhood snack

Tea and Sandwiches

Keep the Sisterhood gingerbread theme going by inviting the girls to use gingerbread cookie cutters (be sure to wash the cutters after using them for the thank-you notes) to make a variety of sisterhood-shaped sandwiches: cucumber and yogurt cheese, cream cheese and olives, ricotta and honey, even old-fashioned PB&J (if no one is allergic)! If any girls have dairy allergies, and no soy allergies, substitute tofu cream cheese, or use any combinations the girls think up that can be spread thinly. Don't forget the tea—go for hot or cold, and green or white (for extra health-promoting antioxidants!).

3 Place the corner where the folds meet at the bottom and trace the triangle's shape on a piece of tracing paper.

4 Draw a girl onto the paper making sure the hands, feet, and skirt are right against the folds.

5 Transfer the drawing to the folded triangle.

6 Cut out the girl, being careful to leave the hands, feet, and skirt edges against the folds.

7 Open up and *voila!* It's a circle of sisterhood!

Then let the girls decide what to say and how (words, images, tiny photos?), and get to it! Their thank-you notes can be sent in the mail, left secretly on someone's desk (like a random act of kindness!), or hand-delivered.

What other ideas might the girls have for giving thanks? Is there a new creative medium they want to try? Remind them that by showing their appreciation to their sisterhood, their sisterhood is more likely to be open to being called on again. That's truly sisterhood working for sisterhood!

Closing Ceremony: Seasoning the Smorgasbord

Gather the girls around their visual Sisterhood Smorgasbord, reminding them that they created this at the start of the journey to represent how they defined sisterhood then. You might say:

Now it's time to adjust the seasonings! Look again at what you created. What might each one of you now add or subtract from this Sisterhood Smorgasbord so that it "tastes" just right?

Looking Ahead to Sessions 9 & 10

The next two sessions are set up for the girls to plan their journey celebration and then carry it out, so think ahead about needed materials by looking through the Sample Sessions ideas.

S'MORE SMORGASBORDS!

If the girls enjoyed reconsidering their Sisterhood Smorgasbord, invite them to take their new views to a more creative level. They might create a new smorgasbord—or a different craft altogether!

Encourage the girls to think about items that they can pass to their wider sisterhood, or to Cadettes bridging to Seniors. Sisterhood bookmarks? Sisterhood mirrors? Sisterhood bracelets? What else?

Thinking back— on all they've learned builds confidence— for the next adventure!

CELEBRATING THE CIRCLE OF SISTERHOOD

SAMPLE SESSIONS 9 & 10
Celebrating the Circle of Sisterhood

HOW BIG A CELEBRATION?

Let the girls decide! Sample Sessions 9 & 10 are combined here so that girls can decide how much they want to plan for their celebration and how and when they will celebrate! Be sure to encourage the girls to make the most of pages 79–80 in their book, which ask them to reflect on all they've learned and accomplished along *Mission: Sisterhood!*

AT A GLANCE

Goal: The Seniors conclude their *MISSION: SISTERHOOD!* journey by discussing what they've learned, connecting with their many sisters, and celebrating mission: accomplished!

● **How Will We Celebrate Our Sisterhood?**

MATERIALS

● Whatever the girls need for celebrating their journey and their accomplishments

PREPARE AHEAD

This Sample Session offers a variety of fun ways to plan and celebrate the journey's close. The girls on your team might want one, two, or even more gatherings to make use of them! Consider these suggestions as possible starting points to guide the Seniors to create their own sisterly ending to their journey, with opportunities to:

● Take pride in what they've learned about friendships and sisterhood, and their collective power

● Share their stories of sisterhood with an expanded network

● Thank all those whom they have met along the journey for their time and insights

● Share their Sisterhood Project(s) with others and see if any ideas emerge about keeping the effort(s) going

● Celebrate among themselves or with whomever they might like to include

● Relax and experience the joy of sisterhood!

How Will We Celebrate Our Sisterhood?

Remind the girls that at the final gathering they will have the chance to celebrate their journey and all that sisterhood has given them. Ask them how they might like to honor one another and their collective accomplishments for sisterhood. Share the following ideas and ask the girls for their own.

SISTERHOOD CEREMONIES

Whether the Seniors have earned their Sisterhood Awards or not, they might take a little time to capture what they've learned and share it with one another. Ceremonies can be a great way to highlight important journey moments.

To get the girls thinking about what they might say during a chosen ceremony, ask them to think about how they'd complete these statements:

- I Discovered that I value . . .
- I will keep living this value by . . .
- When I Connect with the larger sisterhood in my community, I . . .
- I will make more connections by . . .
- I think it is important to Take Action for sisterhood by . . .
- In the future, I'd like to Take Action for sisterhood because . . .
- What does sisterhood do for you? What will you do for it?

LEAVE THE SPECIAL DETAILS TO THE SENIOR SISTERS!

Ask each girl, or small teams of girls, to take responsibility for the special details of their final celebration:

- invitations and possible special guests
- ceremony details
- award ceremony (if earning the Sisterhood Award)
- refreshments
- set up and cleanup crews

SEND OUT INVITES!

Will the Seniors invite guests or is this final celebration for their Senior Circle only?

If guests are planned, encourage the girls to make some creative invitations tied to their celebration theme (maybe even pull out those gingerbread women!).

9 & 10

CELEBRATING THE CIRCLE OF SISTERHOOD

Keep it growing

joy

wisdom

confidence

NAME IT, CREATE IT, SHARE IT!

The girls say one thing they've learned on this MISSION: SISTERHOOD! journey—something about themselves, their friendships, their network, leadership, or a little of each!

Next, the girls capture what they've learned on canvas, through a dance, on film, through a creative recipe, or in any way they can imagine.

Then the girls pass on their joy, wisdom, and confidence by sharing their creation with Girl Scout Cadettes bridging to Seniors. The Seniors encourage the Cadettes to keep the joy, wisdom, and confidence growing! And the Seniors promise to look out for more opportunities to be a leader for sisterhood.

FRIENDSHIP MIXER

Maybe the girls have already done one, or made their Sisterhood Project out of one. Even so, what better way to end their journey than by bringing more women and girls together (see pages 56–57 in the girls' book for specifics).

ONE-ACT PLAY NIGHT

Have the girls share their stories in front of an audience of invited guests (see "Act 'Em Out!" on page 77 in this guide.)

Sisterhood Snack

Celebratory sisterhood snacks

Fresh Friendship-Squeezed Juices: Use citrus of the girls' choice.
Gingerbread Sister Cookies: Bring out that cookie cutter one more time!

Tried-and-True Sisterhood Snacks: Invite the girls to look back over all the snacks they have enjoyed along the journey. Which might they want to serve again?

9&10

CELEBRATING THE CIRCLE OF SISTERHOOD

Now, Celebrate Your Own Circle of Sisterhood!

Now that you have guided girls to expand their sisterhood through leadership, take a moment to think about how these leaders have enriched your life. The Seniors are now part of your sisterhood, and you are part of theirs!

Congratulations!

Now, how will you next expand your sisterhood? Think about that as you ask yourself: So what have I learned about leadership on this journey?

MISSION: SISTERHOOD!
led me to **Discover** that I value

By guiding girls to be
leaders who **Connect** in a larger sisterhood, I

Coaching girls to be leaders who define and **Take Action** on a sisterhood issue taught me

....
....
....

Now I will carry the message of leadership for sisterhood forward by

....
....
....
....
....

way to go, sister!

9 & 10

CELEBRATING THE CIRCLE OF SISTERHOOD

85

NATIONAL LEADERSHIP OUTCOMES

Every experience in this Senior *MISSION: Sisterhood!* journey is designed to help girls be confident leaders in their daily lives—and in the world!

Discover **+** Connect **+** Take Action **=** Leadership

DISCOVER

Girls understand themselves and their values
and use their knowledge and skills to explore the world.

	AT THE SENIOR LEVEL, girls...	RELATED ACTIVITIES (by Session or girls' book chapter/activity)
Girls develop a strong sense of self.	are better able to recognize and address personal and social barriers to reaching personal goals.	S1: *Mission: Sisterhood!* Make It Your Own!; S6&7: Meditation, Closing Ceremonies; S8: Sisterhood Stories; all of S9&10; GB: Ch1: Finesse Your Friendship Style, Measure of Friendship, Finding the Beauty; Ch2: Defining YOU; Ch3: Take Your Friendship Up a Notch; Ch4: Friendship Mixer; Ch5: My Sisterhood Project Planner
	are better able to recognize the multiple demands and expectations of others while establishing their own individuality.	S2: Moving Into Your Social Style; Putting a Value on Friendship, S6&7: Beauty is in the Eye of the Beholder, S8: Sisterhood Stories Take Center Stage, GB: Ch1: Finesse Your Friendship Style, Measure of Friendship, Finding the Beauty in Images of Beauty; Ch2: Defining YOU;
Girls develop positive values.	are better able to recognize and resolve ethical dilemmas.	S3: Further or Fizzle: Friendship Role-Play, S8: Sisterhood Stories Take Center Stage
	strengthen their own and others' commitment to being socially, politically, and environmentally engaged citizens of their communities.	S2: Closing, S3: Creating a Short List, If the Girls Are Stuck; S4: Zeroing in; S5: Planning the Sisterhood Project; S6&7: Coaching Tips; Networking; Closing, S8: Sisterhood Stories; all of S9&10, GB: Earn the Sisterhood Award!, Ch1: Finding the Beauty; Ch2: The Power, Call Out that Inner Beauty!, Ch3: Friendship Mentorship; Ch4: Friendship Mixer; Ch5: Time Capsule, My Sisterhood Project Planner
Girls gain practical life skills—girls practice healthy living.	act as role models for younger girls in making healthy choices.	All Sisterhood Snacks, all of S5: Fit for the Mission, GB: all Science of Sisterhood, Ch2: Body Buddy, Wake-Up Call, Body Talk, Call Out that Inner Beauty!, Ch3: Friendship Mentorship; Ch4: Meditation Breakfast Shake; Keep Safety in Sisterhood, Getting by with a Little Help from Friends
	show cultural sensitivity in their efforts to promote healthy living in their communities.	All Sisterhood Snacks; all of S5; GB: all Science of Sisterhood; Ch2: Body Buddy, Wake-Up Call, Body Talk, Call Out That Inner Beauty!; Ch4: Meditation Breakfast Shake, Keep Safety in Sisterhood
Girls seek challenges in the world.	demonstrate increased enthusiasm for learning new skills and ideas and expanding existing ones.	All of the adult guide and girls' book.
	show increased courage to challenge their own and others' beliefs and opinions.	S1: Creating a Visual Smorgasbord; S4: Zeroing in; S6&7: Beauty Is in the Eye of the Beholder; GB: Ch2: The Power of Sisterhood; Ch3: Take Your Friendship Up a Notch

S=Session, GB=Girls' Book, Ch=Chapter

Girls develop critical thinking.	are better able to analyze their own and others' thinking processes.	S1: Visual Smorgasbord, S2: Moving Into Your Social Style; Putting a Value; Closing Ceremony, S3: Friendships on the Little Screen; What Makes a Great Sisterhood Project?, S4: Zeroing in, S6&7: Beauty is in; Meditation, S8: Closing, GB: Ch1-Measure of Friendship; Be My Own Best Friend, Ch2-Defining YOU; Call Out that Inner Beauty!, Ch3-Take Your Friendship Up, Ch4-In Any Friendship; Tolerance Comes into Play!, Ch5-My Sisterhood Project Planner
	apply critical thinking skills to challenge stereotypes and biases in their lives and in society.	S6&7: Beauty is in the Eye of the Beholder, GB: Ch1-Finding the Beauty in Images of Beauty, Ch2-Call Out that Inner Beauty!, Ch3-Two Friends; a Guide for Many Ch4-In Any Friendship, Tolerance Comes into Play!

CONNECT

Girls care about, inspire, and team with others locally and globally.

	AT THE SENIOR LEVEL, girls...	RELATED ACTIVITIES (by Session or girls' book chapter/activity)
Girls develop healthy relationships.	are better able to recognize and address challenges to forming and maintaining healthy relationships with others.	S2: Putting a Value on Friendship; S3: Further or Fizzle; S4: Modern Game of Telephone, Body Language Charades; GB Ch1: Finesses Your Friendship Style, Measure of Friendship; Ch2: Knowing Your Body Boundaries, Body Talk, Call Out That Inner Beauty!; Ch3: Take Your Friendship Up, Two Friends; Ch4: In Any Friendship, Tolerance Comes into Play!, Friendship Mixer; Ch5: Sisterhood Time Capsule
Girls promote cooperation and team building.	strengthen their abilities to build effective teams to accomplish shared goals.	S1: Creating a Visual Smorgasbord; S3: Creating a Short List, What Makes a Great Sisterhood Project?; S4: Zeroing in; S5: Planning the Sisterhood Project; S6&7: Opening Ceremonies; Coaching Tips: Networking for Sisterhood, S8: Thanking our Sisterhood Circle
Girls feel connected to their communities, locally and globally.	actively seek to bring people together in local and global networks.	S3: What Makes a Great Sisterhood Project? S6&7: Coaching Tips: Networking for Sisterhood; S8: Thanking our Sisterhood Circle; GB: Ch4: Friendship Mixer; Ch5: Sisterhood Time Capsule, Circle Journal, My Sisterhood Project Planner
	feel that their connections with diverse members of their communities are important resources for personal and leadership development.	S6&7: Coaching Tips: Networking for Sisterhood, Meditation, Buddy Button Bracelets; S8: Thanking our Sisterhood Circle; All of S9 &10; GB Ch1: Friendship Potpourri; Ch3: Take Your Friendship Up a Notch, Ch4: In Any Friendship, Tolerance Comes into Play!, Friendship Mixer; Ch5: Sisterhood Time Capsule, Circle Journal, My Sisterhood Project Planner
Girls can resolve conflicts.	can increasingly apply effective strategies for conflict resolution and prevention.	S3: Further or Fizzle: Friendship Role-Play; S4: Zeroing in on a Sisterhood Issue, Modern Game of Telephone, Body Language Charades
	are better able to analyze conflict situations in their communities and globally, and offer possible solutions.	S3: Further or Fizzle: Friendship Role-Play; S8: Sisterhood Stories Take Center Stage
Girls advance diversity in a multicultural world.	are actively engaged in promoting diversity and tolerance.	S6&7: Coaching Tips: Networking for Sisterhood, Meditation, Sisterhood Snack: Diversity Salad; all of S9&10; GB Ch1: Friendship Potpourri; Ch2: Call Out That Inner Beauty!; Ch3: Take Your Friendship Up, Two Friends, a Guide for Many; Ch4: In Any Friendship, Friendship Mixer
	are increasingly able to address challenges to promoting inclusive attitudes and diversity.	S6&7: How Our Network Changed Me; GB: Ch3: Take Your Friendship Up a Notch!, Two Friends, a Guide for Many; Ch4: In Any Friendship, Tolerance Comes into Play!, Friendship Mixer

NATIONAL LEADERSHIP OUTCOMES

TAKE ACTION
Girls act to make the world a better place.

AT THE SENIOR LEVEL, girls...		RELATED ACTIVITIES (by Session or girls' book chapter/activity)
Girls can identify community needs.	are more skilled in identifying their local or global communities' needs that they can realistically address.	S2: Coaching Tips; S3: Creating a Short List for Sisterhood, If the Girls Are Stuck for Project Ideas, What Makes a Great Sisterhood Project?; S4: Zeroing in on a Sisterhood Issue; S5: Planning the Sisterhood Project; S6&7: Coaching Tips: Networking for Sisterhood, GB: Ch5-My Sisterhood Project Planner
	choose Take Action Projects that aim to address deeper causes of issues in their communities.	S2: Coaching Tips; S3: Creating a Short List for Sisterhood, If the Girls are Stuck for Project Ideas, What Makes a Great Sisterhood Project?; S4: Zeroing in on a Sisterhood Issue; S5: Planning the Sisterhood Project; S6&7: Coaching Tips: Networking for Sisterhood, Closing Ceremony; GB: all Expand this Into a Sisterhood Project; Ch5: My Sisterhood Project Planner
Girls are resourceful problem solvers.	are better able to effectively plan and carry out action projects with minimal adult guidance.	S1: Make It Your Own!; S2: Coaching Tips; S3: Creating a Short List, If the Girls are Stuck, What Makes a Great Sisterhood Project?; S4: Zeroing in, S5: Planning the Sisterhood Project; S6&7: Coaching Tips; all of S9&10, GB: all Expand this Into a Sisterhood Project; Ch5: My Sisterhood Project Planner
	are able to assess their progress and adjust strategies as necessary.	S3: What Makes a Great Sisterhood Project?; S4: Zeroing in, S5: Planning the Sisterhood Project; S6&7: Coaching Tips; S8: Sisterhood Stories; GB: Ch5: My Sisterhood Project Planner
Girls advocate for themselves and others.	have increased understanding of how the decisions and policies of various institutions have effects on their lives and the lives of others.	S6&7: Be an Advocate Now, for Girls!, Careers in Advocacy
	use advocacy skills and knowledge to be more active on behalf of a cause, issue or person, locally or globally.	GB: all Expand This into a Sisterhood Project; Ch3: Take Your Friendship Up a Notch!, Ch4: Getting by with a Little Help from Friends; Ch5: My Sisterhood Project Planner
Girls educate and inspire others to act.	are better at inspiring and mobilizing others to become more engaged in community service and action.	S6&7: Coaching Tips: Networking for Sisterhood, Closing Ceremony; S8: Thanking our Sisterhood Circle; GB: all Expand This into a Sisterhood Project; Ch5: Sisterhood Time Capsule, Circle Journal, Keep Your Circle Growing, My Sisterhood Project Planner
Girls feel empowered to make a difference.	are better able to address challenges to their feelings of empowerment.	S4: Opening Ceremony, Closing Ceremony; S6&7: Closing Ceremony; all of S9&10, GB: all Expand This into a Sisterhood Project; Ch2: The Power of Sisterhood to Enforce Boundaries; Ch5: Sisterhood in Action; My Sisterhood Project Planner
	feel that they have greater access to community resources and more equal relationships with adults in their communities.	S6&7: Girls' Appetites Whetted? Give Them More!; S8: Thanking Our Sisterhood Circle; GB: Ch4: In Any Friendship; Ch5: My Sisterhood Project Planner